T0072308

Knowing our
TRIUNE
GOD

RICHARD W. GILBERT

WESTBOW
PRESS®
A DIVISION OF THOMAS NELSON
& ZONDERVAN

This book is a work of non-fiction. Unless otherwise noted, the author and the publisher make no explicit guarantees as to the accuracy of the information contained in this book and in some cases, names of people and places have been altered to protect their privacy.

WestBow Press books may be ordered through booksellers or by contacting:

WestBow Press
A Division of Thomas Nelson & Zondervan
1663 Liberty Drive
Bloomington, IN 47403
www.westbowpress.com
844-714-3454

Because of the dynamic nature of the Internet, any web addresses or links contained in this book may have changed since publication and may no longer be valid. The views expressed in this work are solely those of the author and do not necessarily reflect the views of the publisher, and the publisher hereby disclaims any responsibility for them.

Any people depicted in stock imagery provided by Getty Images are models, and such images are being used for illustrative purposes only. Certain stock imagery © Getty Images.

Scripture quotations are taken from the New American Standard Bible®, Copyright © 1960, 1962, 1963, 1968, 1971, 1972, 1973, 1975, 1977, 1995 by The Lockman Foundation. Used by permission.

ISBN: 979-8-3850-0508-6 (sc)
ISBN: 979-8-3850-0509-3 (e)

Library of Congress Control Number: 2023915198

Print information available on the last page.

WestBow Press rev. date: 08/15/2023

Contents

TRIUNE GOD - THE SON

THE HOLY SPIRIT

Acknowledgements

Throughout all of our years of ministry God has given us the privilege of loving and being loved by two bodies of believers in Western New York: Genesee Country Church and Niagara Frontier Bible Church. Without their prayers, encouragement, questions, and open hearts to receive God's Word these materials would never have been possible.

Very special thanks goes to my wonderful wife who has been my life and ministry partner for all of these years. She has sacrificially enabled me to have the time to pray, study, develop, and write these materials.

Most of all, thank you Heavenly Father for loving me and teaching me even more of who you are. I am overwhelmed by your love, grace, and mercy, and humbled that you would want to use me to teach and proclaim Your Word. May this study help your children to know you more, and through it give to you all the praise, honor, and glory!

Introduction

In the middle of the OT is a book that contains what most Bible scholars have described as wisdom literature. It is a book of Hebrew poetry; actually Hebrew songs: The Book of Psalms; 150 songs written to be sung to ancient tunes played by ancient instruments. Some of the authors are known, like David who wrote the largest number of them; others we know are Solomon, Moses, Asaph, the sons of Korah. In addition to these authors, some of the songs are anonymous, and we will never know who God inspired to pen these words.

While these are Hebrew poetry in their style, they are much more than that; they are the heart expressions of these different authors. These psalms are filled with a breadth of human emotion: fear, uncertainty, anguish, anger, desire for revenge, concern, hope, peace, love, and many other emotions that are all part of our human condition.

As we begin this study about God note what the writers of these psalms say about God and their relationship to him:

> "But you, O Lord, are a shield around me; you
> are my glory, the one who holds my head high. I
> cried out to the Lord, and he answered me from
> his holy mountain. I lay down and slept, yet I

woke up in safety, for the Lord was watching over me" (Psalm 3:3-5).

"Answer me when I call to you, O God who declares me innocent. Free me from my troubles. Have mercy on me and hear my prayer" (Psalm 4:1).

O Lord, our Lord, your majestic name fills the earth! Your glory is higher than the heavens" (Psalm 8:1).

"I know the Lord is always with me. I will not be shaken, for he is right beside me" (Psalm 16:8).

"The Lord is my shepherd; I have all that I need" (Psalm 23:1).

"I love your sanctuary, Lord, the place where your glorious presence dwells" (Psalm 26:8).

"Hear me, Lord, and have mercy on me. Help me, O Lord. You have turned my mourning into joyful dancing. You have taken away my clothes of mourning and clothed me with joy" (Psalm 30:10-11).

"As the deer longs for streams of water, so I long for you, O God. I thirst for God, the living God" (Psalm 42:1-2a).

Some of the psalms in their entirety are about an attribute, a quality, an emotion, a work of God; such as the goodness of God (Psalm 92; 111), the holiness of God (Psalm 99), the power and dominion of God (Psalm 97), the majesty of God (Psalm 93), worship of God (Psalm 84), the fear of God (Psalm 112), and others. The writers of the psalms knew God; not only in their minds (a cognitive recognition of him) and not simply words about him. There was a connection with him at the heart level.

God made man and placed him on this earth so that man could have that level of personal interaction with him. God wants us to have more than a "head knowledge" of him; instead he wants us to have a "heart relationship" with him. He wants us to know him objectively and intimately. He has given us everything that we need for that to be a reality. God wants us to not only know that he loves us, but he wants us to love him back! The more that we know about him, the more that we will love him.

Great appreciation is given to Dr. Alva J. McClain for his work Christian Theology: God and Revelation (Dr. John C. Whitcomb, revision), Floyd Barackman Practical Christian Theology. In addition_J. I. Packer (Knowing God), and Arthur Pink (The Attributes of God) have been consulted and noted throughout.

In this study of God we will first look at those truths that belong corporately to each Person of the Godhead. Then we will individually look at that which is specific to the Father, the Son, and the Holy Spirit. There are two different basic ways in which the subject of God could be approached. One of those ways is the inductive approach, in which different rational arguments for God's existence are presented; ending with the conclusion that God exists. The second way to approach the subject of God is the deductive approach, in which the conclusion statement is made first and then is supported by different facts and observation. This is the way that the Bible presents God, and this is the way that we are going to approach this study.

THEOLOGY
PROPER AND GOD
THE FATHER

GOD EXISTS: THE REALITY OF GOD

Theism is a belief in the existence of a divine reality, belief in the existence of God. Atheism ("a" which means "no" + theism) does not believe that any God, any deity of any kind, exists. A theist believes that everything in the natural world exists because God created it and guarantees its continuance. Christian theism adds that we can personally know the One who has done this; the One who reveals himself as Father, Son, and Holy Spirit.

DEFINITION OF GOD

1. The Bible does not define God, nor does it seek to prove his existence. It begins with the simple declarative statement, "in the beginning God created the heavens and the earth" (Gen 1:1). Nowhere is there an argument in the first biblical book to prove the existence of God; it simply states, "God is."

2. The Bible was written for sinful men who are separated from the One who made them. They don't know who He is, what He is like, what He has done. So, in its very first verse, the Bible brings the reader into the presence of this One they do not know; into the presence of God- "in the beginning God."

3. The clearest simple statement that we can make about God is that he is a living spirit, personal being absolutely distinguished from all other personal beings that he has made by the qualities that he has chosen to reveal about himself.

THE EXISTENCE OF GOD

1. The existence of God is taken for granted in the Bible. "In the beginning God created the heavens and the earth" (Gen. 1:1). Not only that, but it further states "God has spoken." God said, "let there be light" (v.3); "let there be an expanse" (v.6); "let the waters under the heavens be gathered together into one place, and let the dry land appear" (v.9); "then God said...(vv.11, 14, 20, 22, 24, 26, 28, 29)."

2. Man, by his own efforts, cannot prove or disprove the existence of God. The simple fact is that "God is," yet in His grace God has revealed himself to mankind. The apostle Paul in his letter to the believers at Rome wrote, "for the wrath of God is revealed from heaven against all ungodliness and unrighteousness of men who suppress the truth in unrighteousness, because that which is known about God is evident within them; for God made it evident to them. For since the creation of the world His invisible attributes, both His eternal power and divine nature, have been clearly seen, being understood through what has been made, so that they are without excuse" (Rom. 1:18-19).

3. Since Creation, through His creation, God has been revealing himself to mankind. He has been showing mankind his attributes, his power, his nature. All mankind has to do is look around, for everything that has been

made testifies to the existence, nature, and character of the one who made it all, God. Mankind's observations, coupled with his reasoning give good rational arguments for God's existence.

4. There are four primary arguments for God's existence: cosmological argument, teleological argument, anthropological argument, and the ontological argument.

a. Cosmological Argument: Cause

1) Cosmology is the science of the origin and development of the universe. This argument states that there must be a cause for everything. Heb. 3:4 states "for every house is built by someone, but the builder of all things is God." Creation did not come into existence by itself; there must have been a cause.

2) There must have been someone who was capable of making everything and sustaining it. This, of course, is stated in the first verse of the Bible, "in the beginning God created the heavens and the earth." Moses also stated this in Psalm 90, "before the mountains were born or You gave birth to the earth and the world, even from everlasting to everlasting, You are God" (Psalm 90:2).

b. Teleological Argument: Purpose

1) Teleology is the explanation of phenomena by the purpose they serve rather than the cause by which they have come. This argument states the cause of creation a little further. Not only is there a cause of creation, but there is design and purpose in that creation. This argues strongly

against change, spontaneous, or even cataclysmic (Big Bang) creation. Scientific inquiry shows the incredible complexity of even the minutest things in creation.

2) This argument states that the One who created all things is intelligent and had design and purpose in mind as He created things. That intelligent cause of creation is God!

Psalm 19:1 "The heavens are telling of the glory of God; and their expanse is declaring the work of His hands."

Psalm 139:13-14 "For You formed my inward parts; You wove me in my mother's womb. I will give thanks to You, for I am fearfully and wonderfully made; Wonderful are Your works, and my soul knows it very well."

c. Anthropological Argument: Personal component

1) Anthropology is the study of human societies, their cultures and development. Additionally, it is the study of human biological and physiological characteristics and their development. This argument moves the cause of creation beyond a cause with intelligence, design, and purpose and adds to it a personal component.

2) This argument states that mankind is a person with self-awareness and moral self-determination because the One who created him has these qualities.

3) While modern day science and education seek to attribute mankind to evolution, even a slight

cursory examination of man's physical bodies shows the incredible complexity that could only come through the One who made mankind. In addition, the emotional and mental components could only come from One who knows what these are and has them himself.

4) Because God is a person, He has made mankind as persons!

Gen. 1:26-27 "Then God said, 'let us make man in Our image, according to Our likeness; and let them rule over the fish of the sea and over the birds of the sky, and over the cattle and over all the earth, and over every creeping thing that creeps on the earth.' God created man in His own image, in the image of God he created him; male and female He created them."

5) The One who made man a person exists in three persons: Father, Son, and Holy Spirit (Matt. 28:19).

d. Ontological Argument: Existence

1) Ontology is a branch of metaphysics dealing with the nature of being, of existence. Metaphysics is a branch of philosophy that deals with the first principles of things; including abstract concepts, such as being, knowing, substance, cause, identity, time, and space. The ontological argument takes the above arguments one step further, for this one person who has created with design and purpose must exist.

2) When Moses asked God who He was, who is the One sending him back to Egypt, God answered, "I am Who I am" (Exod. 3:14). God said "I am the God who is alive, the living God, the God who exists". God cannot simply be an abstract thought but must actually exist, and He does!

5. These four arguments do not provide scientific proof of the existence of God, but they do show that there must have been some Superior One involved in creation; the One Christians believe is God. Creation gives overwhelming evidence of God's existence. Much of mankind, however, chooses not to accept these facts, and stands guilty before God, their Creator.

NON-CHRISTIAN VIEWS OF GOD

1. Atheism

   A (no) + theism (God).This view denies the existence of any gods.

2. Agnosticism

   A (no) + Gnosticism, from the Greek word *ginosko*; which means "to know". This view states that although he exists, God cannot be known.

3. Polytheism

   This view states that there are many (poly) gods.

4. Zoroastrianism

   This view states that there are two fundamental distinct different realities (good and evil) which oppose one another. It states that at the end of life mankind is judged by God as to whether he/she did more good than evil. Though not identified as this, much of modern liberal theology holds this view.

5. Pantheism

   This view states that everything is an aspect or part of God; God is everything and everything is God.

6. Deism

   This view accepts God's existence but rejects the idea that God has anything to do with the world or what is in it. This view states God made the universe and then stepped away so that it could develop and operate on its own; without any involvement by Him. It denies the Bible being God's Word, but sees it only as a book with good principles.

7. Theism

   This is the view that people have of any god other than that which the Bible shows. They believe in a god, but it is not the One seen in the pages of Scripture; the One who loves mankind and sent His Son to die for man's sins!

GOD CAN BE KNOWN:
THE REVELATION OF GOD

How many times have we said, "I know that it is true, because I have seen it with my own eyes." Someone says that there was a rainbow in the sky. You reply that you also know because you "saw" it yourself. We cannot say, however, that we have seen God, for there is no one today who has seen God. Though we have not seen Him, we can know him. We know God through that which He reveals of himself to mankind.

DEFINITION OF GOD'S REVELATION

Apart from God's revelation of himself, there is nothing that mankind can know about God. Whether that revelation occurs through the creation that man lives in or the Word that God has spoken and written, it would not be there if God had not chosen in his grace to reveal himself to man.

One well-known theologian said, "revelation is a divine activity; not a human achievement. Revelation is not the same thing as discovery or the dawning of insight, or the emerging of a bright idea. Revelation does not mean man finding God, but God finding man; God sharing his secrets with us, God showing us himself" (Packer, 1965, p. 29).

NECESSITY OF GOD'S SELF-REVELATION

1. Psalm 97:9 states, "You are Lord Most High over all the earth; You are exalted far above all gods." Apart from God reaching down to mankind, apart from God taking the initiative and making the way possible, mankind would have no access to God. If God had not spoken to Adam in the Garden, he would never have known that his very existence was from God; would never have known what he was supposed to do. Life would have been mere existence.

2. But God did want man to know where he came from. God did want him to know what he was supposed to do. God did want him to live, not simply exist. God did want him to know that there was hope; there was a remedy for the tragic sinful decision and action they had made and done. God did want a relationship with mankind that He had made. The way that help, hope, understanding, and a relationship with God would come was as God revealed himself to man. That is what He did: through General revelation and Special revelation.

GENERAL REVELATION: IN THE MATERIAL AND ANIMAL CREATION

1. This is what God does continuously for all people through his works or actions in his creation. He made everything and keeps it operating. He provides for mankind and animals; caring for all that He had made.

   a. Job 12:7-10 "Ask the beasts... the birds... the earth, and all will tell you about God: that the hand of the Lord has done this, in whose hand is the life of every living thing, and the breath of all mankind."

11

    b. Acts 14:17 God has given the rains and the seasons as a witness of himself.

    c. Rom. 1:19-20 Since Creation God's attributes, eternal power, and divine nature have been clearly revealed in his creation, so that mankind is without excuse.

2. In Psalm 19:1-6 David (the writer) begins by saying that God reveals himself to mankind through His creation.

    a. Looking into the sky all mankind can see the glory of God; this revelation of God (vv.1-4a).

    b. Looking up, man sees the sun: diameter of 865,000 miles; volume 1 million times that of earth; surface temperature is 5,500 degrees Celsius; one/billionth of its energy reaches our planet. The sun is only one of one trillion + stars in the Milky Way galaxy, and there are many million + galaxies in space.

    c. Looking up, man sees the stars; 100+ billion stars in 100+ billion galaxies; all spoken into existence by God and flung into space by his hand. Not only that, God knows each of them by name (Isa. 40:26)!

3. When we look around we see evidence of God.

    a. God made the seasons: spring, summer, fall, and winter; each for different purposes. Spring brings new life, new birth, and summer brings growth. Fall brings closure to the years growing and harvesting, and winter is a time of rest.

    b. Everywhere and every direction we look we see evidences of God's presence. How do we know that God exists? By what our eyes see! As we look around us, how can we not admit His presence and praise Him?

4. Limitation of this revelation:

   a. While this revelation shows much about God's power and presence, it does not show man's spiritual needs. It does not show mankind his need for salvation, the provision that God has already made for that salvation, and the step of belief that man must take.

   b. It does not show the results of that decision to respond in faith to Jesus Christ, how to live his life as a child of God, and the precious truths of Satan's defeat and Jesus' coming kingdom.

   c. What is needed to see these things is a different kind of revelation, and that is what God has provided.

SPECIAL REVELATION

This is what God has made known to people through his words: his spoken word, his written word, his incarnate Word. Throughout human history God's word has been proclaimed and presented in different ways.

1. God's revelation in direct speech to and with mankind

   a. We see this in God's words to Adam (Gen. 2:16, 18), Noah (Gen. 6:13), Noah's sons (Gen. 9:1, 8), Abram (Gen. 12:1-3), Jeremiah (Jer. 1:4-5), Jonah (Jon. 1:1; 3:1), and numerous others in both testaments.

   b. The Bible does not say how the words came; only that God spoke to them. Much of what we know about God was communicated to man this way. Man was not investigating to find out things about God, but God was choosing to reveal himself to mankind by this means.

13

c. Those to whom God was speaking were seeing and learning more about God, yet that knowledge was limited to those to whom God spoke and those to whom they communicated what they had heard from God.

d. Does God speak directly to people today? No, not normatively, but He can if he chooses to do so.

2. God's revelation in theophanies-visible manifestations of his presence (Gen. 17:1, 18), dreams (Gen. 28:12-13) and visions (Gen. 46:1-4)

a. These occurred as God chose to reveal himself and communicate with mankind in the past.

b. Since we have God's inspired inscribed Word these are not normatively occurring; yet, God can choose, if he desires, to reveal Himself in this manner.

c. God in later Old Testament times spoke through angels (Daniel 9:21), through prophets (2 Kings 1:1-4), the high priest (Num. 27:21), and wise men (1 Kings 13:1-10). During the New Testament times God revealed himself through Jesus (Heb. 1:1-2), through dreams and visions (Matt. 1:20; 2:12, 22).

d. There are many reports of God doing this in many places in today's world.

3. God's revelation in miracles and providential works

a. Miracles are a direct and immediate intervention of God into our physical world to demonstrate to people his power.

1) Exod. 5:1-2; 7:5, 17; 9:14; 10:2- God's direct plagues upon the Egyptians.

2) Num. 14:11 "How long will this people spurn Me? And how long will they not believe in Me, despite all the signs which I have performed in their midst?"

3) Deut. 4:33-35 God did these miracles to show that he is God; that there is no other God. See also Deut. 7:8-9.

4) Joshua 4:23-24 God dried up the Jordan River so the Israelites could cross over, "so that all the peoples of the earth may know that the hand of the Lord is mighty, so that you (Israel) may fear the Lord your God forever."

5) John 10:38 Jesus said to the Jews in the temple who wanted to stone him to death, "if I do the works of my Father (miracles), though you do not believe Me, believe the works (miracles), so that you may know and understand that the Father is in Me, and I in the Father" (John 10:38).

b. Providence is God's indirect usage of natural laws and events to accomplish His will.

1) 2 Kings 20:11 "And Isaiah the prophet called to the Lord, and he brought the shadow back ten steps, by which it had gone down on the steps of Ahaz."

2) Joshua 10:13 "And the sun stood still, and the moon stopped, until the nation took vengeance on their enemies."

3) Isa. 45:1-6 God said prophetically of Cyrus (150 years before the coming events), "I have taken him by the right hand, to subdue nations before him and to loose the loins of kings…that men may know from the rising to the setting of the sun

that there is no one besides Me. I am the Lord, and there is no other."

4) 1 Cor. 10:7-11 Paul said that both these miracles and providences happened as an example and were written for our instruction these many centuries later.

These miracles and providences show that God is true, powerful, righteous, faithful, and concerned about people. They are accessible to all who saw them, but none of them tell the whole story of God's person, power, presence, and love.

4. God's revelation in the Scriptures

a. Heb. 1:1 "God, after He spoke long ago to the fathers in the prophets in many portions and many ways..." The writings of those prophets tell us about God.

b. Luke 24:27 To the two disciples on the Emmaus road, "then beginning with Moses and with all the prophets, He (Jesus) interpreted to them the things concerning Himself in all the Scriptures."

c. John 5:39 "You search the Scriptures because you think that in them you have eternal life; it is these that bear witness about Me."

d. 2 Tim. 3:15 "The Scriptures are able to make you wise unto salvation through faith which is in Christ Jesus."

e. The Scriptures, the Word of God, teach us everything we need to know about God for our salvation. They attest to the person, power, and character of God throughout. Many Old Testament prophecies about Jesus are shown fulfilled in the New Testament.

f. The Scriptures are accessible to all who have a copy and read it; to all who hear it being read and taught. With modern media, God's Word is available for man's reading and hearing across most of the world. At the same time there are still some limitations in translations, literacy, and governmental interference.

5. God's perfect and complete revelation is in Jesus Christ

   a. Matt. 1:23 "Behold, the virgin shall be with child and shall bear a son, and they shall call his name Immanuel, which translated means, 'God with us.'"
   b. Luke 1:31–32 "Mary, you will conceive in your womb and bear a son, and you shall name him Jesus. He will be great and will be called the Son of the Most High."
   c. Matt. 11:27 Jesus said, "no one knows the Son except the Father; nor does anyone know the Father except the Son, and anyone to whom the Son wills to reveal Him."
   d. John 1:14, 18 "And the Word became flesh, and dwelt among us, and we beheld His glory, glory as of the only begotten from the Father, full of grace and truth…No one has seen God at any time; the only begotten God who is in the bosom of the Father, he has explained him."
   e. Heb. 1:2–3 "In these last days spoke to us in his Son, whom he appointed heir of all things, through whom also he made the worlds, who is the radiance of his glory and the exact representation of his nature, and upholds all things by the word of His power."

The revelation of God in Jesus is complete (Col. 2:9–10), perfect (Heb. 1:2–3), and final (John 14:8–9). It is accessible to all who hear and receive the gospel (Rom.

10:13). One day every eye will see him (Rev. 1:7). When God takes us home to heaven we will see Jesus and know more. One day we will see his face (Rev. 22:4), and we will forever be with God!

THE NATURE OF GOD

On the night of his arrest, when Jesus was with his apostles, He said that He will ask the Father to give them another Helper who would be with them forever (John 14:16). That Helper, that Comforter, that *paraklaesis* (Grk), is the Holy Spirit (John 14:17a). Jesus said that while the world does not know Him, the apostles do because He abides with them and will be in them" (v.17b). Jesus said that one of the things the Holy Spirit would do was "to teach them all things, and bring to their remembrance all that He had said to them" (John 14:27).

That specific ministry of the Holy Spirit was not limited to the things that Jesus had said but that He would also teach them "all things." The Holy Spirit is the author of God's Word, all of God's Word; Old Testament and New Testament. Not only would He teach those to whom Jesus was speaking, but he will teach all of God's children. As we come to the Word of God, the author of those words is the One who is going to teach the reader what they say and mean. It is the Holy Spirit who tells us about God; it is the Holy Spirit who helps us understand the nature of God.

GOD HAS THE DIVINE NATURE

Nature has been defined as "the inherent character or basic constitution of a person or thing: essence (Webster's Collegiate

Dictionary, 1994, p.774). The divine nature distinguishes God from other persons. God's nature is very different from that of angels and mankind. While theirs is created, God's is uncreated and underlies all his outward appearances. God's nature is spirit (John 4:24). God does not have a tangible body as mankind does; no physical presence that we can see with our eyes or touch with our hands.

When Moses asked to see God's glory, God said that no one could see His face and live, but he would put Moses in a cleft in the rock and pass by; allowing Moses to see his back (Exod. 33:19-23). Moses does not tell what he saw on the mountain that day as God showed him His glory.

The closest description that we can get of God is Ezekiel's description of what he saw in his vision of the Four Living Beings and the Divine Glory (Ezek. 1). After describing the Four Living Beings Ezekiel said,

> "Now over the heads of the living beings there was something like an expanse, like the awesome gleam of crystal, spread out over their heads. Under the expanse their wings were stretched out straight, one toward the other; each one also had two wings covering its body on the one side and on the other. I also heard the sound of their wings like the sound of abundant waters as they went, like the voice of the Almighty, a sound of tumult like the sound of an army camp; whenever they stood still, they dropped their wings. And there came a voice from above the expanse that was over their heads; whenever they stood still, they dropped their wings.

"Now above the expanse that was over their heads there was something resembling a throne, like lapis lazuli in appearance (deep blue); and on that which resembled a throne, high up, was a figure with the appearance of a man. Then I noticed from the appearance of His loins and upward something like glowing metal that looked like fire all around within it, and from the appearance of His loins and downward I saw something like fire; and there was a radiance around Him. As the appearance of the rainbow in the clouds on a rainy day, so was the appearance of the surrounding radiance. Such was the appearance of the likeness of the glory of the Lord. And when I saw it, I fell on my face and heard a voice speaking" (Ezek. 1:22-28).

GOD IS A PERSON

What are the qualities, characteristics, components that define or encompass being a person or personhood? While God exists as three distinct Persons, each of whom is totally, wholly, Deity, each has these characteristics or components which define their personhood. At least eight of these can be expressed: life, intelligence, purpose, activity, freedom, self-consciousness, emotion, spirituality (intangibility), volition. Note, there is no mention of a corporeal body. Personhood does not require a body which then responds in some way to these characteristics. God the Father and the Holy Spirit do not have bodies, while God the Son took upon himself a human body at the incarnation in Mary and remains in bodily form for all eternity.

God is not merely a concept, a force of energy, a power, or the combination of everything as pantheism suggests. God is a person who lives, thinks, acts with purpose and will; a person who sees, hears, speaks, loves, is angry, blesses people, judges people. Because God is a person, we can talk to him and know that he hears us. We can tell him about the things that are occurring and know that he understands. Because God is a person, we can ask him to help us with that which we are experiencing. Because God is a person we can trust him, know him, love him, worship him, serve him .

For millennia mankind has tried to do this with statues/idols they have made, but none of them has been able to respond, because they are not persons. They are only pieces of wood, stone, metal that have been shaped into an image. They are not persons; only inanimate objects. God, however, is a person and responds to all He sees, hears, and knows.

Isaiah writes of the folly of idolatry; shaping wood into the form of a man so that it can sit in a house (Isa. 44:13). He plants a tree, burns part of it over a fire to keep warm and then shapes the other half into a god and bows down in worship before it (vv.14-17). His eyes are blinded so that he cannot see, and his heart is not able to comprehend his error (vv.18-20). All of the gods that the surrounding nations were worshipping, all the gods of all the nations are lifeless, inanimate statues and images. Only God is a person; as we now see a "living" person.

GOD IS SPIRIT

Spirit in the New Testament is the name describing the source or center of personality, whether God, angels, or mankind. Spirit is not personality, but it is that which describes the core essence of a person."

When Jesus' followers saw him after his resurrection, they were terrified because they thought he was a spirit. He calmed their fears by saying, "Why are you troubled, and why do doubts arise in your hearts? See My hands and My feet, that it is I Myself; touch Me and see, for a spirit does not have flesh and bones as you see that I have" (Luke 24:38-39). Spirit is nonmaterial, noncorporeal; thus God is not composed of material, corporeal parts. While "no one has seen God at any time" (John 1:18a), God has given visions or revelations of himself (Exod. 33:18-34:9 and Ezek. 1:22-28).

> Zech. 4:6 "Then he said to me, 'this is the word of the Lord to Zerubbabel saying, Not by might nor by power, but by My Spirit, says the Lord of hosts."

> John 4:24 "God is spirit, and those who worship Him must worship in spirit and truth."

> Heb. 12:9b "Shall we not much rather be subject to the Father of spirits and live?"

GOD IS LIVING

Life in the Bible simply means "potential energy or activity;" being able to do something, not necessarily doing it. God is able to speak (Deut. 5:26), able to work miracles (Josh. 3:10-17), able to deliver his people (Dan. 6:26-27), able to judge and punish those who do evil (Heb. 10:30-31). God is not only able to do things, but He also does them.

> Deut. 5:26 "Who is there of all flesh who has heard the voice of the living God speaking from the midst of the fire, as we have, and lived?"

The sons of Korah wrote, "How lovely are your dwelling places, O Lord of hosts! My soul longed and even yearned for the courts of the Lord. My heart and my flesh sing for joy to the living God" (Psa. 84:1-2).

1 Tim. 4:10 "We have fixed our hope on the living God, who is the Savior of all men, especially of believers."

Luke 24:10 "Why do you seek the Living One among the dead?"

GOD IS INTELLIGENT

God's intelligence/wisdom is a warning to sinners; He knows what and why he is doing things (1 Sam. 2:3). It is also an encouragement and hope to the Godly (Job 23:10- He knows what he is doing).

1 Sam. 2:3 "The Lord is a God of knowledge, and with Him actions are weighed".

Psalm 139:1-6 God knows everything.

Prov. 2:6 "For the Lord gives wisdom; from His mouth come knowledge and understanding."

Rom. 11:33 "Oh, the depth of the riches both of the wisdom and knowledge of God! How unsearchable are his judgments and unfathomable his ways!"

1 John 3:20 "God is greater than our heart and knows all things."

Prov. 3:19-20 "The Lord by wisdom founded the earth, by understanding he established the heavens. By his knowledge the deeps were broken up and the skies drip with dew." God spoke Creation into existence. God knew what He wanted to come into existence, what it was to look like, how it was to act or function, the minute details of complexity and operation, how it was to exist and function in relationship to other things or entities, and millions and millions of other details. The longer science probes the complexities of space, human anatomy, the microscopic and atomic world, the more they are faced with the reality of not only intelligent design, but that only God could do these things.

GOD IS PURPOSIVE/VOLITIONAL

This is having, serving, or doing something with a purpose; reacting to a future goal (Websters New Collegiate Dictionary, 1993, p.949). Purpose is a distinctive mark of personality because it is found only in mankind, angels, and God. Here plans and preparations are made with a future goal in mind.

At creation God had a specific plan for how He was going to do things. As we look at the sequential days of creation, it is easy to see why the individual things were done in both the time period and order presented. Mankind was made on day six according to God's plan and purpose; the woman was made for the man because of God's specific purpose. God is not capricious, reactionary, or random. He acts according to his plans and purposes.

> Eph. 3:11 Referring to Gentiles and Jews saved by grace; revealed to the angelic world- "This was in accordance with the eternal purpose which He carried out in Christ Jesus our Lord."

Isa. 14:26 "This is the plan devised against the whole earth; and this is the hand that is stretched out against all the nations." God determined what, when, and how he was going to deal with Assyria. God is not reactionary like we are but always has a purpose and plan for what he is doing.

Gal. 4:4-5 "But when the fullness of the time came, God sent forth His Son, born of a woman, born under the Law, so that He might redeem those who were under the Law, that we might receive the adoption as sons."

Being purposive includes volition. Volition, the ability to choose, is an essential element or component of personhood. A robot is programmed to respond in a certain way to different stimuli, physical or electronic impulses. The same programming is readily seen in computers, electronic games, etc. People, angelic beings, God are able to make a choice of how they are going to respond. Lucifer and one-third of the angelic realm chose to rebel against God. Adam and Eve chose to disobey God. Man everyday makes hundreds, even thousands of choices of how he is going to respond to different things. God chooses what He is going to do, going to say, how He will respond to anything and everything occurring. Not only is God free, as we have already seen, but He can and does make choices!

GOD IS ACTIVE

Deism states that God exists, but He does not have anything to do with the world or what is in it. Its position is that God is inactive in relationship to anything in this world. That makes Him no different than the columns in Athens that the apostle Paul saw (Acts 17) or the inanimate lifeless idols that people were worshipping. That is in absolute contrast to all that we see of God in relationship to anything and everything in this world.

When God was sending Moses back to Egypt to deliver the Jewish people from their bondage in that nation, He said, "I know that the king of Egypt will not permit you to go, except under compulsion. So I will stretch out My hand and strike Egypt with all My miracles which I shall do in the midst of it; and after that he will let you go" (Exod. 3:19-20).

> Psalm 92:4-5 "For You, O Lord, have made me glad by what You have done, I will sing for joy at the works of your hands. How great are Your works, O Lord!"

> Prov. 3:5-6 "Trust in the Lord with all your heart and do not lean on your own understanding. In all your ways acknowledge Him, and he will make your paths straight."

> Daniel 6:27 "He delivers and rescues and performs signs and wonders in heaven and on earth, Who has also delivered Daniel from the power of the lions."

> John 5:17 Jesus said, "My Father is working until now, and I Myself am working."

> Phil. 2:13 "For it is God who is at work in you, both to will and to work for His good pleasure."

GOD IS FREE

Nothing external causes or directs God to any decision or action. All of his actions are determined only by His nature and choice.

> Job 23:13 Job said of God, "He is unique and who can turn Him? And what His soul desires, that He does."

> Exod. 33:19 God said to Moses, "I will have mercy on whom I will have mercy, and I will have compassion on whom I will have compassion." See also Rom. 9:15.

> Psalm 115:3 "Our God is in the heavens; He does whatever he pleases."

> Daniel 4:35 "All the inhabitants of the earth are accounted as nothing, but He does according to His will in the host of heaven and among the inhabitants of earth; and no one can ward off His hand or say to Him, 'what have You done?'"

> 1 Cor. 12:18 "But now God has placed the members, each one of them, in the body, just as he desired."

> Eph. 1:11-12 "We have obtained an inheritance, having been predestined according to His purpose who works all things after the counsel of His will, to the end that we who were the first to hope in Christ would be to the praise of His glory."

GOD IS SELF-CONSCIOUS

We see this self-consciousness readily in mankind. As a baby grows it becomes more aware of itself; finding and exploring their fingers, toes, nose, voice. That same self-consciousness is perfectly seen and revealed in God. When Moses asked who he should say sent him to Egypt, God said "I am who I am" (Exod. 3:14).

Mankind's self-consciousness is only partial. He doesn't know how sinful he is (Psalm 139:23-24), thinking that some of the good things he has and does are OK, but they aren't (Isa. 64:6). But God knows himself completely. 1 Cor. 2:11 "For who among men knows the thoughts of a man except the spirit of the man which is in him? Even so the thoughts of God no one knows except the Spirit of God."

> Isa. 55:8-9 "For my thoughts are not your thoughts, neither are your ways my ways, declares the Lord. For as the heavens are higher than the earth, so are my ways higher than your ways and my thoughts than your thoughts."

> Jer. 29:11 "For I know the thoughts that I think toward you, saith the Lord, thoughts of peace, and not of evil, to give you an expected end" (KJV).

GOD IS EMOTIONAL

God's emotions are not mere human emotions/feelings projected onto Him. God has these emotions, and when he made mankind he put these same emotions into his creation. When God made the first man and woman, the emotions in them were pure, just as God's emotions are pure, sinless. Since mankind's sin in the Garden of Eden man's condition has changed. Now mankind is born with a sinful human nature and those emotions are affected by our sinful nature. Even those who have come to faith in Christ are affected by their "flesh" (old nature), and their emotions are touched by that sinfulness!

> Deut. 5:9 "You shall not worship them (idols) or serve them; for I, the Lord your God, am a jealous God, visiting the iniquity of the fathers on the children, and on the third and the fourth generations of those who hate Me." JEALOUSY

> Judges 10:16 "So they put away the foreign gods from among them and served the Lord; and He could bear the misery of Israel no longer. GRIEF

> Psalm 5:5 "The boastful shall not stand before Your eyes; You hate all who do iniquity." HATRED

> Psalm 103:13 "Just as a father has compassion on his children, so the Lord has compassion on those who fear him." COMPASSION

> Isa. 62:5 "For as a young man marries a virgin, so your sons will marry you; and as the bridegroom rejoices over the bride, so your God will rejoice over you." REJOICING

> Isa. 63:8-9a "For He said, 'surely, they are My people, sons who will not deal falsely.' So, He became their Savior. In all their affliction He was afflicted." SUFFERING

Jer. 31:3"The Lord appeared to him from afar saying, 'I have loved you with an everlasting love; therefore I have drawn you with lovingkindness." LOVE

Luke 19:41 "When He approached Jerusalem, He saw the city and wept over it." COMPASSION

John 3:16 "For God so loved the world, that he gave His only begotten Son." LOVE

Rom. 1:18 "For the wrath of God is revealed from heaven against all ungodliness and unrighteousness of men who suppress the truth in unrighteousness." WRATH

THE UNITY OF GOD

The nation of Israel existed in the midst of many nations who worshipped a multitude of gods. Abram, the father of the Jews, most likely worshipped the gods of his countrymen when he left Ur of the Chaldees and went to Haran with his father Terah (Gen. 11:31). There in Haran, after Terah died, God spoke to Abram and told him to go to the land that He (God) would show him. There Abram would begin to know that only God was God. Centuries later, after enslavement in Egypt for 430 years, Moses led the descendants of Abram (Abraham) out of that slavery to freedom in the land of Canaan.

When they arrived in the Sinai wilderness, God spoke to them from the top of the mountain. There would be no question in their minds after these first words from God to them. For all to hear, God said, "I am the Lord your God, who brought you out of the land of Egypt, out of the house of slavery. You shall have no other gods before me. You shall not make for yourself an idol, or any likeness of what is in heaven above or on the earth beneath or in the water under the earth. You shall not worship them or serve them…" (Exod. 20:1-5a). During those 40 years in the wilderness the Israelites would learn and believe that only God (Jehovah) is God, and that all those other gods of all the nations are only the creation of men's minds and hands.

From these Old Testament Scriptures we see that only God is God:

> Deut. 4:32-39 "To you it was shown that you might know that the Lord, he is God; there is no other besides Him (v.35)…Know therefore today and take it to your heart, that the Lord, He is God in heaven above and on the earth below; there is no other" (v.39).

> Deut. 6:4-5 "Hear, O Israel! The Lord is our God, the Lord is one! You shall love the Lord your God with all your heart and with all your soul and with all your might."

> Isa. 44:6-8 "Thus says the Lord, the King of Israel and his Redeemer, the Lord of hosts: 'I am the first and I am the last, and there is no God besides me. Who is like Me? Let him proclaim and declare it; Yes, let him recount it to me in order, from the time that I established the ancient nation. And let them declare to them the things that are coming and the events that are going to take place. Do not tremble and do not be afraid; Have I not long since announced it to you and declare it? And you

are My witnesses. Is there any God besides Me, or
is there any other rock? I know of none!"

Isa. 45:5-6 "I am the Lord, and there is no other;
beside me there is no God. I will gird you, though
you have not known Me; that men may know
from the rising to the setting of the sun that there
is no one besides Me. I am the Lord, and there is
no other."

We see these New Testament Scriptures also attesting to the unity
of God:

John 5:44 Jesus answering those complaining
because he healed the lame man on the Sabbath
(5:19-47) said, "how can you believe, when you
receive glory from one another and you do not
seek the glory that is from the one and only God?"

John 10:30 Jesus said, "I and the Father are one."

Rom. 3:29-30 "Is God the God of Jews only?
Is he not the God of Gentiles also? Yes, of
Gentiles also, since indeed God who will justify
the circumcised by faith and the uncircumcised
through faith is one."

God the Father is God (John 20:17); God the Son
is God (John 1:1, 14; Rom. 9:5); God the Holy
Spirit is God (Acts 5:3-4; 1 Cor. 3:16).

TRIUNITY OF GOD

The word "triunity" of God comes from the Latin *tri* (3) + *unus* (1); thus 3 in 1. The more common word for it is "Trinity". This doctrine states that God is one; existing as three eternal, simultaneous persons: the Father, the Son, and the Holy Spirit.

God is one God because there is only one divine nature (essence), which is undivided and indivisible. While the unity of God stresses the Oneness of God, the Triunity (trinity) of God states there are three separate persons possessing the divine nature. The Trinity consists of three simultaneous, coexistent, eternal Persons- the Father, Son, and Holy Spirit. We see this presented in Matt 28:19.

FALSE VIEWS OF THE TRINITY

The early church did not have a clear understanding of the Trinity. It was when heretical and false views of the relationship among the Godhead began to surface in the church that they saw the need to define and carefully present what they knew to be the truth. It was in the church councils that these false and heretical views were examined and shown to be the lies and distorted views they actually were.

1. Sabellianism

    This is also called Modal Monarchianism. It was taught in Rome by Sabellius (A.D. 215). This view states that God is a monad, an ultimate unit of being that expresses itself in three consecutive operational manifestations: the Father as essence, the Son and Holy Spirit as modes of self-expression for the Father. These projections of the Father are temporary, not simultaneous; the Father projects himself as the son, and at another time as the Holy Spirit. The Bible, in clear opposition to this view states the members of the godhead are distinct, eternal, coexistent Persons.

2. Arianism

Arius was a presbyter in Alexandria, Egypt in the 4th century AD. Arius believed that there is only one God, God the Father. He further believed that the Son is a personal creature that the father created out of nothing, and he believed that the Holy Spirit is an impersonal essence very different from the Father. Arius later amended his view of the Holy Spirit and said that He was created by the Son at the Father's request. The Bible teaches that the Son and Holy Spirit are God, just as the Father is God; all being equal in their essential qualities.

3. Tritheism

This view states that the Trinity consists of three separate divine essences; thus, not only one God but three! The Bible teaches that there is only one God; existing in three distinct, eternal Persons, each one being God.

Some of these ancient heresies are still in existence today. The United Pentecostal Movement today believes the deity of the Father, Son, and Holy Spirit, but denies they are distinct, coexistent Persons: Sabellianism. The Jehovah's Witnesses deny the deity of Jesus Christ and the deity of the Holy Spirit: Arianism.

THE OLD TESTAMENT AND THE TRINITY

A number of Old Testament texts suggest more than one person in the Godhead.

1. There is one God (Deut. 6:4; Isa. 45:5-6, 18, 22).

   Deut. 6:4 states, "Hear, O Israel: the Lord (*Yahweh*- Heb.) is our God, the Lord (*Yahweh*) is one (*ehad*- Heb.).

   When Moses asked God to show him His glory, God said, "I myself will make all My goodness pass before you and will proclaim the name of the Lord before you" (Exod 33:19a). God descended onto Mt. Sinai and revealed himself to Moses, and as He did so he said, "the Lord (*Yahweh*), the Lord (*Yahweh*) God (*El*-Heb.), Exod 34:6.

   God's name is Lord (Yahweh). Additionally, the Deut. 6:4 passage states that He is one (*ehad*). While the word "*ehad*" translated "one" stresses singleness, it also stresses diversity within that oneness (TWOT, I, p.30). Some translations bring this out more clearly as "the Lord is our God, the Lord alone." There is only one God, and His name is Yahweh.

2. Use of the plural name of God: Elohim

   Gen. 1:1 "in the beginning God created the heaven and the earth." The name for God in this verse is Elohim, which is the plural name for God.

   Deut. 6:4 "the Lord (*Yahweh*) is our God (*Elohim*).

   Both verses help us to see the plurality of the Godhead. Elohim is the plural form of the word El, which is the generic name for Deity. See "Elohim" in God's Names in the Old Testament later in this resource. While he alone is God, he is more than one person. The use of the plural name of God is not there by mistake but was deliberately chosen by the author of the Bible: the Holy Spirit.

3. Plural pronouns are used of God

    Gen. 1:26 "let Us make man in Our image."

    Gen. 3:22 "Then the Lord God said, 'behold, the man has become like one of Us."

    Gen. 11:7 "Come, let Us go down and there confuse their language."

    Isa. 6:8 "Whom shall I send, and who will go for Us?

4. God's name is applied to more than one person in the same text

    Psalm 2:7 "I will surely tell of the decree of the Lord: He said to Me, 'You are My son, today I have begotten You."

    Psalm 45:6-7 "Your throne, O God, is forever and ever; a scepter of uprightness is the scepter of Your Kingdom. You have loved righteousness and hated wickedness; therefore God, Your God, has anointed you with the oil of joy above Your fellows." This is quoted in Heb. 1:8-9.

    Psalm 110:1 "The Lord says to my Lord: sit at My right hand until I make Your enemies a footstool for Your feet."

    Prov. 30:4 Speaking of the Holy One (God), "what is His name or His son's name?"

Jer. 23:5-6 "Behold the days are coming, declares the Lord, when I will raise up for David a righteous Branch… and this is His name by which He will be called, The Lord our righteousness."

5. The three persons of the Godhead are given in Isa. 48:16; 61:1; the Son speaking in each passage.

Isa. 48:16 "…and now the Lord God has sent Me, and His Spirit."

Isa. 61:1 "The Spirit of the Lord God is upon me, because the Lord has anointed me to bring good news to the afflicted; He has sent Me to bind up the brokenhearted, and to proclaim liberty to captives and freedom to prisoners."

Each member of the Godhead is God. The Father is called LORD (Psa. 110:1); The Father and Son are called God (Psa. 45:6-7; Heb. 1:8-9). The Son is called God (Isa. 7:14). Jer. 31:33-34 is God the Father making a New Covenant with the Israelites; Heb. 10: 15-16 tells us that it is the Holy Spirit who is doing this.

THE NEW TESTAMENT AND THE TRINITY

1. In the New Testament three persons appear, and each of them is recognized as God.

One of these is called Father- John 6:27 "Do not work for the food which perishes, but for the food which endures to eternal life, which the Son of Man will give to you, for on Him the Father, God, has set his seal."

A second is called the Son – Heb. 1:8 "But of the Son He says, 'Your throne, O God, is forever and ever.'"

A third is called the Holy Spirit- Acts 5:3-4 speaking to Ananias, Peter said, "why has Satan filled your heart to lie to the Holy Spirit…You have not lied to men but to God."

2. Each of these three persons is clearly distinguished from the others

    Luke 1:35 "The Holy Spirit will come upon you, and the power of the Most High will overshadow you; and for that reason the holy Child shall be called the Son of God."

    John 14:16, 26 Jesus said, "I will ask the Father, and he will give you another Helper, that He may be with you forever; that is the Spirit of truth…the Helper, the Holy Spirit, whom the Father will send in My name."

    John 15:26 "When the Helper comes, whom I will send to you from the Father, that is the Spirit of truth who proceeds from the Father, He will testify about Me."

3. These three Persons are presented as one God, not three Gods.

    John 10:30 Jesus said, "I and the Father are one."

    1 Cor. 2:11 "the thoughts of God no one knows except the Spirit of God." Father and Spirit are one.

    John 14:16, 18, 23 The Father, Son, and Spirit are one.

4. These three are equal in being, power, and glory

   Each of these is called "God."

   They are associated with one another in a way consistent with equality.

   Matt. 28:19 "Go therefore and make disciples of all the nations, baptizing them in the name of the Father and the Son and the Holy Spirit."

   2 Cor. 13:14 "The grace of the Lord Jesus Christ, and the love of God, and the fellowship of the Holy Spirit be with you all."

5. There is no specific order in which the Persons of the Godhead are presented.

   They are all equal in Deity, and the order of their presentation is not important.

   2 Thess. 2:13-14 Father- Spirit-Christ

   Eph. 4:4-6 Spirit- Christ- Father

   Jude 20-21 Spirit- Father- Christ

These are vital teachings for the Church, the Body of Christ. In A.D. 589 the Church met at the Council of Toledo (Spain) to discuss who sent the Holy Spirit; was it the Father or the Father and Son together. The Catholics believed the Father and Son sent the Holy Spirit. The Greek Orthodox believed that only the Father sent the Holy Spirit. This was known as the Filioque Controversy, and the church split over this issue.

THE ATTRIBUTES OF GOD

How are we to describe God? What is he like? What are those qualities, characteristics, attributes, those essential qualities that belong to and reveal His nature? They are not separate from him but instead essential components, descriptors that help us to understand and know him.

There are different ways in which God's attributes are classified. Some have classified them based upon moral and non-moral qualities. Some have classified them upon God's relationship with the universe: absolute and relative, or transitive and intransitive, some as communicable and incommunicable. Chafer said, "the attributes of God present a theme so vast and complex and so beyond the range of finite faculties that any attempt to classify them must be only approximate as to accuracy or completeness. Also the attributes are so interrelated and interdependent that the exact placing of some of them is difficult if not wholly impossible" (Chafer, 1980, vol.1, p.189).

For purpose of presentation and discussion this study will seek to look at God's attributes under two major groupings; though anything said about them is woefully insignificant and failing to describe what God is like. These two groupings are (1) God's Greatness, and (2) God's Goodness. Those attributes presented under God's greatness are Eternal, Unchangeable, Omnipresent,

Omniscient, Omnipotent, Perfect, Infinite, Incomprehensible, Sovereign. Those attributes presented under God's goodness are Holy, True, Love, Righteous, Faithful, Merciful, Just, Gracious.

ATTRIBUTES OF GOD'S GREATNESS

GOD IS INFINITE

The English word translated "infinite" occurs only in Psalm 147:5 "Great is our Lord and abundant in strength; His understanding is infinite." The Hebrew word used there "no number". There is no number large enough to measure God. To say that God is infinite means that He is completely without limits; with the exception of those he has imposed upon himself. He is not shut-in by what we call nature but is infinitely exalted above it. God limited himself in the way he entered mankind in Christ; in the way he created the universe.

When King Solomon dedicated the temple that he had built for God, he said, "will God indeed dwell on the earth? Behold, heaven and the highest heaven cannot contain You, how much less this house which I have built" (1 Kings 8:27).

In Matt. 13:58 we read, "And he did not do many miracles there because of their unbelief." Their unbelief did not prevent Jesus from doing miracles, but because they would not believe God chose not to do them. Because of their unbelief many would not even come to Jesus to seek healing.

Notice how infiniteness is so descriptive of what God is like.

> Psalm 40:5 "Many, O Lord, my God, are the wonders which You have done, and Your thoughts toward us; There is none to compare with you.

If I would declare and speak of them, they would be too numerous to count."

Psalm 71:15 "My mouth shall tell of Your righteousness and of Your salvation all day long; for I do not know the sum of them."

Psalm 89:2 "For I have said, Lovingkindness will be built up forever; in the heavens You will establish Your faithfulness."

Psalm 103:12 "As far as the east is from the west, so far has he removed our transgressions from us."

Job 5:9 "Who does great things and unsearchable, wonders without number."

God's infiniteness is a comfort to His people. There is nothing that we face in this life that is too great for God.

John 1:50 "Jesus answered, and said to him, 'because I said to you that I saw you under the fig tree, do you believe? You will see greater things than these.'" There is no limit to what God can do, and He will as He chooses.

God's infiniteness is a warning to the wicked.

Psalm 51:4 David said, "against You, You only, I have sinned and done what is evil in Your sight, so that You are justified when You speak and blameless when You judge." David's sin, and every sin, is not merely a little sin or simply against another person; it is ultimately against God who is infinite!

John 3:36 "He who believes in the Son has eternal
life; but he who does not obey the Son will not
see life, but the wrath of God abides on him."
God's wrath is against those who do not believe
on, who reject Jesus Christ who is infinite!

GOD IS ETERNAL

The Bible begins with this simple statement, "in the beginning
God created the heavens and the earth" (Gen. 1:1). This is the
beginning of creation. At a point in time past God spoke things
into existence, and then we see him making things through
his direct touch. While this was the beginning of time, God
was already there! All of creation: spiritual things and material
things have a beginning; a point in time when they were brought
into existence. Angels and mankind will live forever; they have
everlasting life, and it will be either with God or forever separated
from him. All of creation had a beginning and will never have
an end. But God alone is eternal; he had no beginning and will
have no end.

Deut. 32:40 God said, "Indeed, I lift up My hand
to heaven, and say, as I live forever."

Gen. 21:33 "Abraham planted a tamarisk tree at
Beersheba, and there he called on the name of the
Lord, the Everlasting God."

Deut. 33:27a "The eternal God is a dwelling
place, and underneath are the everlasting arms."

Psalm 90:1-2 "Lord, You have been our dwelling
place in all generations. Before the mountains
were born or You gave birth to the earth and the

world, even from everlasting to everlasting, You are God."

Psalm 102:12 "But You, O Lord, abide forever, and your name to all generations."

Isa. 9:6 "and his name will be called Wonderful, Counselor, Mighty God, Eternal Father, Prince of Peace."

Isa. 57:15 "For thus says the high and exalted One who lives forever, whose name is Holy: I dwell on a high and holy place, and also with the contrite and lowly of spirit in order to revive the spirit of the lowly and to revive the heart of the contrite."

Hab. 1:12a "Art You not from everlasting, O Lord, my God, my Holy One?"

Rom. 1:20 "For since the creation of the world His invisible attributes, His eternal power and divine nature, have been clearly seen..."

1 Tim. 1:17 "Now to the King eternal, immortal, invisible, the only God, be honor and glory forever and ever. Amen."

Rev. 1:8 "I am Alpha and Omega, says the Lord, who is, and who was, and who is to come, the Almighty."

Rev. 4:10 "the four and twenty elders will fall down before him who sits on the throne, and will worship him who lives forever and ever, and will cast their crowns before the throne."

God's existence cannot be measured by time (Psalm 90:1-2); He is above time (Isa. 57:15); and He is both the author and ruler of time (Heb. 1:2; 1 Tim. 1:17; Isa. 9:6).

Because God is eternal we can trust His promises, because He will always be here to fulfill them. Because God is eternal we know that we will not be alone, for God is here with us each new day. Because God is eternal we have hope and help for God knows the future and will be here with us as that future becomes today. Because God is eternal we know that what God said would happen will happen, because God will be there to make it happen. Because God is eternal we have help that will never fail us!

GOD IS UNCHANGEABLE (IMMUTABLE)

Immutability means that there is no change in God's nature, character, mind, or will. He never becomes greater or less. He never grows, learns, develops, improves, evolves, or ages. There can be changes in his actions, which are always in accordance with his will. God character does not change, but his response to man will vary in response to men's actions.

<u>God does not change His nature</u>

Exod. 3:14 "God said to Moses,' I am who I am.'"

Num. 23:19 "God is not a man, that he should lie; nor a son of man, that he should repent. Has he not said, and he will not do it? Or has he spoken, and will he not make good?"

Mal. 3:6 "For I, the Lord, do not change; therefore you, O sons of Jacob, are not consumed."

James 1:17 "Every good thing given and every perfect gift is from above, coming down from the Father of lights, with whom there is no variation or shifting shadow."

God does not change His Word

God's Word is truth, and it will never change. In a world that says truth is relative, God says that it is fixed, absolute, unchangeable; because He is unchangeable!

Psalm 33:11 "The counsel of the Lord stands forever, the plans of his heart from generation to generation."

Psalm 119:160 "The sum of Your word is truth, and every one of Your righteous ordinances is everlasting."

Psalm 110:4 "The Lord hath sworn, and will not change His mind, You are a priest forever according to the order of Melchizedek."

Matt. 5:18 "For truly I say to you, until heaven and earth pass away, not the smallest letter or stroke shall pass from the Law until all is accomplished."

John 17:17 Jesus said of the disciples, "sanctify them in the truth; Your Word is truth."

God does not change His will

God does change how he deals with mankind; relative to how they respond to his commands and warnings. He didn't bring judgment upon the people of Nineveh when they repented (Jonah 3), but He did send Israel and later Judah into captivity when they didn't repent.

> Ezek. 24:14 "I, the Lord, have spoken; it is coming and I will act. I will not relent, and I will not pity and I will not be sorry; according to your ways and according to your deeds I will judge you," declares the Lord God."

> Jer. 26:13 "Now therefore amend your ways and your deeds and obey the voice of the Lord your God; and the Lord will change His mind about the misfortune which He has pronounced against you."

GOD IS OMNISCIENT
God's Knowledge Includes Everything

His knowledge is without limits; knowing everything past, present, and future! "For if our heart condemn us, God is greater than our heart, and knows all things" (1 John 3:20).

God's knows all things in the material world.

> Job 28:24 "For he looks to the ends of the earth, and sees everything under the whole heaven."

> Psalm 147:4 "He counts the number of the stars; he gives names to all of them."

God knows all things in the animal world.

> Matt. 10:29 "Are not two sparrows sold for a cent? And yet not one of them will fall to the ground apart from your Father." God is deeply involved with animal's actions.

God knows the spirit world of the dead.

> Job 26:6 "Naked is Sheol before him, and Abaddon has no covering." God knows perfectly and intricately everything that is happening in our world and in the spirit world.

God knows the world of mankind.

> Psalm 33:13-15 "The Lord looks from heaven; He sees all the sons of men; from His dwelling place He looks out on all the inhabitants of the earth, He who fashions the hearts of them all, He who understands all their works."

> Acts 1:24 Choosing who was to be the replacement for Judas Iscariot, "they prayed, and said, 'You, Lord who know the hearts of all men, show which of these two You have chosen."

God knows all the details of personal life.

> Psalm 139:1-4 "O Lord, You have searched me and known me, You know when I sit down and when I rise up; You understand my thought from afar. You scrutinize my path and my lying down, and are intimately acquainted with all my

ways. Even before there is a word on my tongue, Behold, O Lord, You know it all."

Psalm 139:15 "My frame was not hidden from You, when I was made in secret, and skillfully wrought in the depths of the earth."

Prov. 5:21 "For the ways of a man are before the eyes of the Lord, and he watches all his paths."

Jer. 1:5 "Before I formed you in the womb I knew you, and before you were born I consecrated you."

Matt. 10:30 "But the very hairs of your head are all numbered."

God knows all past and future events .

Isa. 46:9-11 "Remember the former things long past, for I am God, and there is no other; I am God, and there is no one like Me, declaring the end from the beginning, and from ancient times things which have not been done, saying, 'My purpose will be established, and I will accomplish all My good pleasure; calling a bird of prey from the east, the man of My purpose from a far country (Cyrus the Persian). Truly I have spoken; truly I will bring it to pass. I have planned it, surely I will do it."

God knows all possible events under all possible combinations of circumstances.

Matt. 11:21 "Woe to you, Chorazin! Woe to you, Bethsaida! For if the miracles had occurred in Tyre and Sidon which occurred in you, they would have repented long ago in sackcloth and ashes."

God's Knowledge is Eternal, Perfect (without errors), and Complete

Acts 15:18 "Says the Lord, who makes these things known from long ago."

Job 37:16 Elihu questioning Job, "do you know about the layers of the thick clouds, the wonders of one perfect in knowledge."

Heb. 4:13 "And there is no creature hidden from His sight, but all things are open and laid bare to the eyes of Him with whom we have to do,"

God's Knowledge Involves Moral Purpose

Prov. 15:3 "The eyes of the Lord are in every place, watching the evil and the good."

God's knowledge is a comfort and consolation to His people. Hagar was greatly encouraged by the reality that God saw her condition and helped her (Gen. 16:13). The psalmist was encouraged by the fact that God knew of his wanderings and tears and that God had a record of them (Psalm 56:8). Jesus said that our Father knows what we need even before we ask him (Matt. 6:8).

God's knowledge is a warning to the wicked. God sees what the wicked are planning and doing, and he will judge them (Psalm

94:3-9). God sees both the good and evil that is done (Prov. 15:3), and he will judge it.

All who are mortal must at some point say that they do not know. Only one, God, always knows, and because of that only He will always lead us in the right direction and to the right decision. As we trust and rest in Him, we will have hope, contentment, and His peace in our hearts!

GOD IS OMNIPOTENT

Jeremiah gives the summary statement of God's power: "Ah Lord God! Behold, You have made the heavens and the earth by Your great power and by Your outstretched arm! Nothing is too difficult for You" (Jer. 32:17).

There are no limitations on God's power. Jehoshaphat's prayer further supports these words: "O Lord, the God of our fathers, are you not God in the heavens? And are You not ruler over all the kingdoms of the nations? Power and might are in Your hand so that no one can stand against You" (2 Chron. 20:6).

These additional verses should be viewed as one begins consideration of God's omnipotence.

> Gen. 17:1 "Now when Abram was ninety-nine years old, the Lord appeared to Abram and said to him, 'I am God Almighty (El Shaddai)' walk before me, and be blameless.'"

> Gen. 18:14 "Is anything too difficult for the Lord: At the appointed time I will return to you, at this time next year, and Sarah will have a son."

Num. 11:23 Regarding food for the Israelites, "the Lord said to Moses, 'is the Lord's power limited? Now you shall see whether My word will come true for you or not.'"

Job 42:1-2 "Job answered the Lord, and said, I know that You can do all things, and that no purpose of Yours can be thwarted."

Rev. 19:6 "Then I heard something like the voice of a great multitude and like the sound of many waters and like the sound of mighty peals of thunder, saying, 'Hallelujah! For the Lord our God, the Almighty, reigns.'"

God is Able To Do All Things Consistent with His Nature and Character

2 Tim. 1:13 "If we are faithless, He remains faithful, for he cannot deny Himself."

Titus 1:2 "In hope of eternal life, which God, who cannot lie, promised ages ago."

James 1:13 "Let no one say when he is tempted, 'I am being tempted by God;' for God cannot be tempted by evil, and he Himself does not tempt anyone."

God is Never Tired, Never Exhausted by the Exercise of His Power

Isa. 40:28 "Do you not know? Have you not heard? The Everlasting God, the Lord, the Creator of the ends of the earth does not become weary or tired. His understanding is inscrutable. He gives strength to the weary, and to him who lacks might he increases power."

God's Power is Seen in...

1. Creation

   Jer. 10:12 "It is He who made the earth by His power, who established the world by His wisdom; and by His understanding he has stretched out the heavens."

2. Nature

   Jer. 10:13 "When He utters His voice, there is a tumult of waters in the heavens, and he causes the clouds to ascend from the end of the earth; He makes lightning for the rain, and brings out the wind from His storehouses."

3. History

   Dan. 4:17 "This sentence is by the decree of the angelic watchers and the decision is a command of the holy ones, in order that the living may know that the Most High is ruler over the realm of mankind, and bestows it on whom He wishes and sets over it the lowliest of men."

4. Heaven

   Dan. 4:35 "All the inhabitants of the earth are accounted as nothing, but He does according to His will in the host of heaven and among the inhabitants of earth; and no one can ward off His hand or say to Him, 'what have You done?'"

5. Redemption

> Eph. 1:18-19 "I pray that the eyes of your heart may be enlightened, so that you will know what is the hope of His calling, what are the riches of the glory of His inheritance in the saints, and what is the surpassing greatness of His power toward us who believe."

What are the practical values of this attribute? As we walk through this world, we do not need to fear, for God is greater than anything we face. While difficulties, problems, and struggles will be there, we can face and be victorious over all of them in God's strength. The psalmist said, "I have set the Lord continually before me; because He is at my right hand, I will not be shaken" (Psa. 16:8). Hallelujah! For the Lord our God, the Almighty, reigns (Rev. 19:6)!

GOD IS OMNIPRESENT

Pantheism states that God is everything, but the Bible tells us that God is the Creator of everything. There is a vast difference between these two views. The doctrine of God's omnipresence states that God is in the universe; everywhere present at the same time. At the same time, however, God is greater than the universe. Psalm 113:6 states God has to humble himself to look in the universe. A clearer statement is that everything is in God's presence. These verses speak of God's omnipresence:

> 1 Kings 8:27 Solomon's prayer at the dedication of the temple, "But will God indeed dwell on the earth? Behold, heaven and the highest heaven cannot contain You, how much less this house which I have built!"

Isa. 57:15 "For thus says the high and exalted One who lives forever, whose name is Holy,' I dwell on a high and holy place, and also with the contrite and lowly of spirit in order to revive the spirit of the lowly and to revive the heart of the contrite.'"

Jer. 23:23-24 "'Am I a God who is near,' declares the Lord, 'and not a God far off? Can a man hide himself in hiding places so I do not see him?' declares the Lord. 'Do I not fill the heavens and the earth?' declares the Lord."

Psalm 139:7-12 "Where can I go from Your Spirit? Or where can I flee from Your presence? If I ascend to heaven, You are there. If I make my bed in Sheol, behold, You are there. If I take the wings of the dawn, if I dwell in the remotest part of the sea, even there Your hand will lead me, and Your right hand will lay hold of me. If I say, 'surely the darkness will overwhelm me, and the light around me will be night,' even the darkness is not dark to You, and the night is as bright as the day. Darkness and light are alike to you."

Acts 17:26b-28a To the Athenians on Mars Hill Paul said, God "made from one man every nation of mankind to live on all the face of the earth, having determined their appointed times and the boundaries of their habitation, that they would seek God, if perhaps they might grope for Him and find Him, though he is not far from each one of us; for in Him we live and move and exist."

There is no place we can go that God is not there; from the highest mountain to the deepest valley; on the moon or under the earth; in the greatest joy or the deepest sorrow; in complete safety or deepest danger. Wherever we are and whatever is happening in our lives, God is there!

GOD IS PERFECT

The Hebrew word translated "perfect" is *tamim* and means perfect, complete, full, whole, without blemish (Brown-Driver-Briggs Lexicon, 1980, p.1070). The Greek word translated "perfect" is *teleios* and means perfect in the sense of completed or finished (Bauer-Arndt-Gingrich-Danker Lexicon, 1979, p.809). To say that God is perfect means that He is complete, lacking nothing, he is in complete accordance with what the Bible states as criteria for a God.

1. God Himself is perfect

    Matt. 5:48 "Therefore you are to be perfect, as your heavenly Father is perfect."

2. God's work is perfect

    Deut. 32:3-4 "For I proclaim the name of the Lord; ascribe greatness to our God! The Rock! His work is perfect, for all His ways are just; a God of faithfulness and without injustice, righteous and upright is He." God is perfect by His holy righteousness standards, not the flawed standards of the world.

3. God's knowledge is perfect

    Job 37:16 Elihu questioning Job, "do you know about the layers of the thick clouds, the wonders of one perfect in knowledge?"

4. God's way is perfect

    Psalm 18:30 "As for God, His way is blameless (KJV-perfect); the word of the Lord is tried; He is a shield to all who take refuge in Him."

5. God's Law is perfect

    Psalm 19:7 "The law of the Lord is perfect, restoring the soul; the testimony of the Lord is sure, making wise the simple."

6. God's will is perfect

    Rom. 12:2 "And do not be conformed to this world, but be transformed by the renewing of your mind, so that you may prove what the will of God is, that which is good and acceptable and perfect."

7. God's gifts are perfect

    James 1:17 "Every good thing given and every perfect gift is from above, coming down from the Father of lights, with whom there is no variation or shifting shadow."

God's perfection means that all we need is found in him. Col. 2:10 "And in Him you have been made complete (NIV "given fullness), and He is the head over all rule and authority."

The Bible does state that God's creation was very good (Gen. 1:31). Satan himself was described as perfect in beauty (Ezek. 28:12). Noah (Gen. 6:) and Job (Job 1:1) are described as blameless before God. They were spiritually right before God, but they were not perfect. Only God is absolutely perfect!

GOD IS INCOMPREHENSIBLE

God's incomprehensibleness means that He cannot be comprehended by any finite mind; neither human or angelic. These verses speak of this attribute of God:

> Job 5:9 "Who does great and unsearchable things, wonders without number."

> Job 11:7-8 "Can you discover the depths of God? Can you discover the limits of the Almighty? They are high as the heavens, what can you do; deeper than Sheol, what can you know?"

> Psalm 145:3 "Great is the Lord, and highly to be praised, and His greatness is unsearchable."

> Isa. 40:28 "Do you not know? Have you not heard? The Everlasting God, the Lord, the Creator of the ends of the earth does not become weary or tired, His understanding is inscrutable." Inscrutable means impossible to understand or interpret.

> Rom. 11:33 "Oh, the depth of the riches both of the wisdom and knowledge of God! How unsearchable are his judgments and unfathomable His ways!"

While God is incomprehensible, that does not mean that he is unknowable. Much can be known about God. Jesus, in his prayer in the Upper Room said to his Father, "this is eternal life, that they may know You, the only true God, and Jesus Christ whom You have sent" (John 17:3).

The apostle Paul wrote, "for who has known the mind of the Lord, that he will instruct him?" (1 Cor. 2:16). That did not stop him from desiring and taking steps to know Him more: "that I may know Him and the power of his resurrection and the fellowship of His sufferings, being conformed to His death" (Phil. 3:10).

1 John 4:7 "Beloved, let us love one another; for love is from God, and everyone who loves is born of God and knows God." Our love for one another is evidence that we have been born again. Because of that we can know more about God and know him more experientially!

ATTRIBUTES OF GOD'S GOODNESS

Scripture clearly states that God is good; seen in this small selection of verses.

Psalm 25:8 "Good and upright is the Lord; therefore He instructs sinners in the way."

Psalm 31:19 "How great is Your goodness, which You have stored up for those who fear You, which You have wrought for those who take refuge in You, before the sons of men!"

Psalm 52:1 "Why do you boast in evil, O mighty man? The lovingkindness of God endures all day long."

Psalm 65:4 "How blessed is the one whom You choose and bring near to You to dwell in Your courts. We will be satisfied with the goodness of Your house, your holy Temple."

Psalm 145:7-10 "They shall eagerly utter the memory of Your abundant goodness and will shout joyfully of Your righteousness. The Lord is gracious and merciful; slow to anger and great in lovingkindness. The Lord is good to all, and His mercies are over all His works. All Your works shall give thanks to You, O Lord, and your godly ones shall bless You."

Mark 10:18 "And Jesus said to him, 'why do you call Me good? No one is good except God alone."

Rom. 2:4 "Do you think lightly of the riches of His kindness and tolerance and patience, not knowing that the kindness of God leads you to repentance?"

Rom. 11:22 "Behold then the kindness and severity of God; to those who fell, severity, but to you, God's kindness, if you continue in His kindness; otherwise you also will be cut off."

When we look at the goodness of God, the attributes that are classified and considered here fall into two categories: (1) those attributes which describe what God is in himself (Holy, Truth,

Love, Righteous); (2) those attributes which describe what God is in relation to others (Faithful, Mercy, Grace).

GOD IS HOLY

<u>Scripture statements of God's holiness:</u>

1. God's people must be holy

   Lev. 11:45 "For I am the Lord who brought you up from the land of Egypt to be your God; thus you shall be holy, for I am holy."

2. Things devoted to God are holy

   Lev. 27:28 "Nevertheless, anything which a man sets apart to the Lord out of all that he has, of man or animal or of the fields of his own property, shall not be sold or redeemed. Anything devoted to destruction is most holy to the Lord."

3. God's habitation is holy

   Deut. 26:15 "Look down from Your holy habitation, from heaven, and bless Your people Israel."

4. God's throne is holy

   Psalm 47:8 "God reigns over the nations, God sits on His holy throne."

5. God's Spirit is holy

   Psalm 51:11 "Do not cast me away from Your presence and do not take Your Holy Spirit from me."

6. God swears by His holiness

   Psalm 89:35 "Once I have sworn by My holiness; I will not lie to David."

7. God's holy arm

   Psalm 98:1"O sing to the Lord a new song, for he has done wonderful things, His right hand and His holy arm have gained the victory for Him."

8. God's holy Word

   Psalm 105:42 "For He remembered His holy word with Abraham His servant."

9. God's name is holy

   Isa. 57:15 "For thus says the high and exalted One who lives forever, whose name is Holy."

10. God is worshipped because He is holy

    Isa. 6:1-5 Seraphim cry "holy, holy, holy" to God.

    Psalm 99:1-9 The entire psalm speaks of God's holiness.

Meaning of the words translated "holy"

The English word "holy" essentially means "whole." Its usage means "wholly pure in a moral sense; devoted to a sacred purpose." The Hebrew word *qadosh* and the Greek word *hagios* essentially mean the same thing: separateness, set apart (Brown-Driver-Briggs, 1980, p.871 and Bauer-Arndt-Gingrich-Danker, 1979, p.9). From these words, it is easy to see the necessity of moral purity for the child of God. "For God has not called us for the purpose of impurity, but in sanctification" (King James Version, "unto holiness")- 1 Thess. 4:7.

Meaning of the holiness of God

Holiness is the very center of all that God is. He is absolutely separate; set apart as we see in the following descriptors.

1. God is absolutely separate from all that is earthly or created. His is a holiness of Divine Majesty.

   Psalm 99:1-3 God is holy because he is separate from everyone.

   Isa. 57:15 God is above and beyond the universe; that is why he is holy!

2. God is absolutely separate from all that is morally unclean. His is a holiness of Moral Purity.

   Psalm 99:4-9 Because He executes righteousness and justice, He is holy.

   Psalm 24:3-4 "Who may ascend into the hill of the Lord? And who may stand in His holy place? He who has clean hands and a pure heart, who has not lifted up his soul to falsehood."

3. Everything that God does; all of His acts are holy.

The fundamental moral attribute is holiness

The Bible seems to make holiness the basic or foundational attribute of God's goodness.

Isa. 6:1-3 "I saw the Lord sitting on a throne, lofty and exalted, with the train of his robe filling the temple. Seraphim stood above Him, each having six wings: with two he covered his face, and with two he covered his feet, and with two he flew. And one called out to another and said, 'Holy, Holy, Holy, is the Lord of hosts. The whole earth is full of His glory.'"

Isa. 57:15 In the Old Testament names meant something, often describing something about the person. In this verse Isaiah states that God's name is holy, and that he dwells on a high and holy place.

Psalm 47:8 "God reigns over the nations, God sits on His holy throne." God's rule, government, is holy.

Practical Values of God's holiness

1. God's holiness guarantees the unchangeableness (immutability) of his covenants.

   Psalm 89:34-36 God will always keep His promise because he is holy.

   Psalm 105:42 God remembered his holy word to Abraham.

   John 17:11 Jesus asked His Father to keep His children in His name; keep them because of who He is!

2. God's holiness reveals our uncleanness. It confronts us with the sinfulness of our sin.

When Isaiah saw the Lord seated upon his throne and the seraphim crying out holy, holy, holy, he was overcome with the reality of his own sinfulness: "woe is me, for I am ruined! Because I am a man of unclean lips, and I live among a people of unclean lips; for my eyes have seen the King, the Lord of hosts" (Isa. 6:5). Every sin is against God (Psalm 51:4).

3. God's holiness demands holiness in His people.

God's holiness is not merely academic, but it is essential to who we are. The holiness of God must be at the center of how we make sense of our lives. Mankind was made in the image of God and with the first man was absolutely holy. When sin came that all changed, but God in his grace reached out and chose a man (Abraham) and to his descendants said they were to be holy. When they disobeyed him, God judged them because he is holy (Psalm 99:8-9). If God is not holy, all we would have is despair.

The apostle Peter tells those who have trusted Christ as Savior that we are to be holy because he is holy (1 Peter 1:15-16); that is to be the ultimate quest of our lives. The writer of Hebrews tells his readers that "God disciplines us for our good, so that we may share in His holiness" (Heb. 12:10). God works to produce that holiness in us.

4. God holiness guarantees the ethical nature of our salvation.

Psalm 98:1 "O sing to the Lord a new song, for he has done wonderful things, His right hand and His holy arm have gained the victory for Him."

5. God's holiness reveals the character of the coming Kingdom; causing us to long for a world ruled by Him.

   Psalm 47:8 "God reigns over the nations, God sits on His holy throne."

   Isa. 11:9 describing conditions during the Millennial reign of Christ, "they will not hurt or destroy in all My holy mountain, for the earth will be full of the knowledge of the Lord as the waters cover the sea."

6. God's holiness is the background (and precipitant) of his Divine judgment.

   Rev. 20:11 Jesus seated on the Great white throne

7. God's holiness is an encouragement to believers today.

   Isa. 57:15 God not only dwells on a high and holy place, but "also with the contrite and lowly of spirit in order to revive the spirit of the lowly and to revive the heart of the contrite." Not only is God in the high and holy place, but he is also with those who have lost hope and those who are repentant.

GOD IS TRUTH (TRUENESS OF GOD)

Scripture Statement

1. He is the true God.

   John 17:3 Jesus' prayer- "This is eternal life, that they may know You, the only true God, and Jesus Christ whom You have sent."

1 Thess. 1:9 "you turned to God from idols to serve a living and true God."

The trueness of God means that He conforms exactly to the highest possible ideal of what God ought to be. When Jesus said he was the only true God he was saying that His Father was genuine, not an impostor or one somewhat similar; He is the One who is truly God!

2. He is the truthful God.

John 17:17 "Jesus' prayer-"sanctify them in the truth; your word is truth."

Psalm 119:160 "the sum of Your word is truth, and every one of Your righteous ordinances is everlasting."

Psalm 19:9 "The judgments of the Lord are true; they are righteous altogether."

God's knowledge and words speak to things exactly as they are.

3. He is the God of truth.

Psalm 31:5 "Into Your hand I commit my spirit; You have ransomed me, O Lord, God of truth."

Isa. 65:16 "Because he who is blessed in the earth will be blessed by the God of truth; and he who swears in the earth will swear by the God of truth…"

John 14:6 Jesus said, "I am…the truth."

All truth is grounded in his being and nature. Everything that is true is true because God made it that way.

Relationship of God's trueness to other attributes

Exod. 34:6 God proclaimed to Moses, "the Lord, the Lord God, compassionate and gracious, slow to anger, and abounding in lovingkindness and truth."

2 Sam. 2:6 David said, "now may the Lord show lovingkindness and truth to you."

Psalm 111:8 God's precepts are "performed in truth and uprightness."

Jer. 4:2 "As the Lord lives, in truth, in justice and in righteousness."

Jer. 33:6 "I will bring to this city (Jerusalem) health and healing, and I will heal them; and I will reveal to them an abundance of peace and truth."

John 1:17 "Grace and truth were realized through Jesus Christ."

John 14:6 Jesus said, "I am the Way, the Truth, and the Life."

With each of these attributes above, they belong to the One who is the God of truth; therefore each is all that they should be because of who God is: He is TRUE!

God's trueness …

1. Assures us that God will respond to all true worship and prayer (John 4:23-24; Psalm 145:18).
2. It guarantees that God will keep all his promises (Jer. 4:2).
3. Guarantees that God's final judgment will be just .

Rom. 2:2 "We know that the judgment of God rightly falls upon those who practice such things."

4. Guarantees he will never prove unworthy of trust.

Psalm 31:5 "Into your hands I commit my spirit; You have ransomed me, O Lord, God of truth."

GOD IS LOVE

Scripture Statement

1 John 4:7-8 "Beloved, let us love one another, for love is from God; and everyone who loves is born of God and knows God. The one who does not love does not know God, for God is love." LOVE IS THE VERY ESSENCE OF GOD'S BEING

Isa. 49:14-16 "But Zion said, 'the Lord has forsaken me, and the Lord has forgotten me.' Can a woman forget her nursing child and have no compassion on the son of her womb? Even these may forget, but I will not forget you. Behold, I have inscribed you on the palms of My hands; Your walls are continually before Me.'" GOD'S LOVE NEVER FORGETS

Isa. 63:7-9 "In all their affliction He was afflicted, and the angel of His presence saved them; In His love and in His mercy He redeemed them, and He lifted them and carried them all the days of old." GOD'S LOVE IS ACTIVE

Jer. 31:3 "The Lord appeared to him from afar, saying, 'I have loved you with an everlasting love; therefore I have drawn you with lovingkindness." GOD'S LOVE IS THE REASON FOR HIS KINDNESS

Psalm 103:11 "For as high as the heavens are above the earth, so great is His lovingkindness (steadfast love) toward those who fear Him." GOD'S LOVE IS IMMEASURABLE

John 3:16 "For God so loved the world, that he gave His only begotten Son, that whoever believes in Him shall not perish, but have eternal life." GOD'S LOVE GIVES SACRIFICIALLY

1 John 4:7-10 "Beloved, let us love one another, for love is from God; and everyone who loves is born of God and knows God. The one who does not love does not know God, for God is love. By this the love of God was manifested in us, that God has sent His only begotten Son into the world so that we might live through Him. In this is love, not that we loved God, but that he loved us and sent His Son to be the propitiation for our sins." GOD'S SACRIFICIAL LOVE

The doctrine is the same in both testaments. While the object of his love in the O.T. is primarily Israel, it is not exclusively to Israel. God's love extends to all the families of the earth (Gen. 12:1-3). God's love includes all men; God loved the people in Nineveh and sent Jonah to preach to them (Jonah 4:11). God's love is "that in him which moves Him to give Himself and His gifts spontaneously, voluntarily, righteously, and eternally for the good of personal beings, regardless of their merit or response" (Whitcomb, God and Revelation, 1982, p.72). Love is much more than an emotion; it is an action.

God's Love is Unselfish

There is no thinking about personal benefit, but God's love seeks only the good of the recipient.

Deut. 7:7-8 "The Lord did not set His love on you nor choose you because you were more in number than any of the peoples, for you were the fewest of all peoples, but because the Lord loved you and kept the oath which He swore to your forefathers, the Lord brought you out by a mighty hand and redeemed you from the house of slavery, from the hand of Pharaoh king of Egypt." God's love was based on the promises and covenants He had already given them.

God's Love is Voluntary

God does not wait for a request before he expresses or demonstrates His love. He chooses where, when, and how to grant his love.

Hosea 3:1 "Then the Lord said to me, 'Go again, love a woman who is loved by her husband, yet an adulteress, even as the Lord loves the sons of Israel, though they turn to other gods and love raisin cakes.'"

Hosea 14:4 Of Israel God said, "I will heal their apostasy, I will love them freely, for My anger has turned away from them."

Rom. 5:8 "But God demonstrates His own love toward us, in that while we were yet sinners, Christ died for us."

1 John 4:10 "In this is love, not that we loved God, but that he loved us and sent His Son to be the propitiation for our sins."

God's Love is Righteous; Never Condones Sin

Psalm 11:7 "For the Lord is righteous, He loves righteousness; the upright will behold His face."

God's Love is Everlasting; Endures Forever

Jer. 31:3 "The Lord appeared to him from afar, saying, 'I have loved you with an everlasting love; therefore I have drawn you with lovingkindness."

Rom. 8:38-39 "For I am convinced that neither death, nor life, nor angels, nor principalities, nor things present, nor things to come, nor powers, nor height, nor depth, nor any other created thing, will be able to separate us from the love of God, which is in Christ Jesus our Lord."

Who Does God Love?

1. God loves His only-begotten Son.

    Matt. 3:17 At Jesus' Baptism God said, "this is My beloved Son..."

    Matt. 17:5 At Jesus' transfiguration God said, "this is My beloved Son..."

    John 3:35 "The Father loves the Son and has given all things into His hand."

2. God loves those who love the Son and believe on Him.

    John 16:27 "For the Father Himself loves you, because you have loved Me and have believed that I came forth from the Father."

    1 John 3:1 "See how great a love the Father has bestowed on us, that we would be called children of God; and such we are. For this reason the world does not know us, because it did not know Him."

3. God loves the nation of Israel.

    Jer. 31:3-4 To Israel God said, "I have loved you with an everlasting love.

    Zeph. 3:17 Concerning Israel …"The Lord your God is in your midst, a victorious warrior. He will exult over you with joy, He will be quiet in His love, He will rejoice over you with shouts of joy."

4. God loves the world and every person in it.

    John 3:16 "For so loved the world that He gave His only begotten Son…" God's love does not negate his other attributes, so even though God loves mankind, he does not simply overlook mankind's sin. Man must receive Jesus Christ by faith. God's love is seen in his grace and mercy extended to mankind.

How is God's Love Seen?

1. It is seen in doing good impartially to all men.

    Matt. 5:43-44 "You have heard that it was said, 'you shall love your neighbor and hate your enemy.' But I say to you, love your enemies and pray for those who persecute you."

    1 Tim. 4:10 "We have fixed our hope on the living God, who is the Savior of all men, especially of believers."

2. It is seen in giving Himself for the objects of his love.

    John 3:16 "For God so loved the world, that he gave His only begotten Son, that whoever believes in Him shall not perish, but have eternal life."

3. In suffering with and for the objects of His love.

   Judg. 10:16 God was grieved; "could bear the misery of Israel no longer."

   Psalm 68:19 "Blessed be the Lord, who daily bears our burden, the God who is our salvation."

   Isa. 63:9 "In all their affliction he was afflicted, and the angel of His presence saved them; in his love and in His mercy he redeemed them, and he lifted them and carried them all the days of old."

4. In dying for the objects of his love.

   Rom. 5:8 "God demonstrates His own love toward us, in that while we were yet sinners, Christ died for us."

5. In His hatred of all that evil

   Psalm 45:7 God hates wickedness.

6. In disciplining His own children

   Prov. 3:12 "For whom the Lord loves he reproves, even as a father corrects the son in whom he delights."

   Heb. 12:5-8 Do not regard lightly the Lord's discipline, "for those whom the Lord loves he disciplines..."

Our Response to God's Love

1. It demands a loving response on our part.

   1 John 4:11 Since God loves us, we are to love one another.

2. It produces a response in us toward God and his people.

    1 John 4:19 We love him because He first loved us.

3. It is an evidence of our salvation.

    1 John 2:10 "The one who loves his brother abides in the Light and there is no cause for stumbling in him."

    1 John 3:14 "We know that we have passed out of death into life, because we love the brethren. He who does not love abides in death."

    1 John 4:7 'Beloved, let us love one another, for love is from God; and everyone who loves is born of God and knows God."

    1 John 4:11-12 "If we love one another, God abides in us, and his love is perfected in us."

4. God's love works in us; preparing us for the Day of Judgement.

    1 John 4:15-18 God's love in us is preparing us for the day when we will stand before Jesus Christ, and we will have nothing to fear!

GOD IS RIGHTEOUS

The words that Scripture uses to present and describe this are "just, justice, right, righteous, righteousness."

General Biblical Testimony of God's Righteousness

Psalm 11:7 "For the Lord is righteous, He loves righteousness; the upright will behold His face."

Psalm 19:8 "The precepts of the Lord are right, rejoicing the heart..."

Psalm 45:6 "Your throne, O God, is forever and ever; a scepter of uprightness is the scepter of Your kingdom."

Psalm 89:14 "Righteousness and justice are the foundation of Your throne; lovingkindness and truth go before You."

Psalm 119:137 "Righteous are You, O Lord, and upright are Your judgments."

Psalm 145:17 "The Lord is righteous in all His ways and kind in all His deeds."

Jer. 50:7 "They have sinned against the Lord who is the habitation of righteousness."

Two Kinds of Divine Righteousness

As we come to the righteousness of God we find it presented in two different ways in Scripture. One of these is the righteousness of God demonstrated and accomplished by the death of Christ which can be given to sinners. The other is the righteousness of God which is an attribute of His character and is non-transferable (Whitcomb, 1982, p.75). Both of these are seen in Rom. 3:21-26.

The key word to understand in the first of these, the righteousness of Christ given to sinners, is "imputation." The word "impute" means "to reckon over into one's account" (Unger, 1988, p.612).

Paul's words to Philemon about Onesimus the runaway slave illustrates the meaning of imputation: "charge that to my account" (Philem. 18).

Imputation is seen in these ways as we consider the righteousness of Christ given to sinful man. Adam's sin was imputed to the whole human race (Rom. 5:12). Because all mankind sinned through Adam, death spread to all mankind. We see also that the only remedy for mankind's sin was Jesus Christ: the sin of the human race was imputed to Christ. This was a legal (forensic) transference of man's sin onto Christ. Isaiah spoke of this when he said, "the chastening for our well-being fell on him...the Lord has caused the iniquity of us all to fall on him" (Isa. 53:5-6). Paul wrote of Jesus, "God made Him who knew no sin to be sin on our behalf, so that we might become the righteousness of God in Him" (2 Cor. 5:21).

This leads us to the righteousness of God that is imputed to the believer. Jesus took upon himself our sin; became sin for us so that we could be righteous before God. The only way that sinful man can stand in acceptance before Holy God is that he is seen as righteous. That occurs as man responds in faith to Christ and as a result the righteousness of God, through Christ's sacrifice, is imputed to man. It is this righteousness from God which alone allows us into the presence of God (Phil. 3:9). That righteousness is ours as Paul states, "even the righteousness of God through faith in Jesus Christ for those who believe" (Rom. 3:22).

In addition to the righteousness of Christ which is given to sinners, God's righteousness is also presented as an attribute of His character. It is this righteousness that Paul states next in Rom.3:25-26, "this was to demonstrate His righteousness, because in the forbearance of God he passed over the sins previously committed; for the demonstration, I say, of His righteousness at the present time, so that he would be just and the justifier of the one who has faith in Jesus."

Nature of God's Righteousness

The Hebrew word for righteousness, *sedek*, means "straight" (Brown-Driver-Briggs, 1980, p.841), while the Greek word for righteousness, *dikaiosunae*, means " what God requires; what is right, righteous, good, just, right" (Bauer-Arndt-Gingrich-Danker,1979, p. 196). When used of God it means that he is absolutely free from any unrighteousness: Psalm 92:15 "To declare that the Lord is upright; He is my rock, and there is no unrighteousness in Him." God's righteousness is above any righteousness that man says that he has or thinks that he has. Man would know nothing of God's righteousness if God was not revealing it to him (John 17:25).

Manifestation/Revealation of God's Righteousness

How is God's righteousness seen in his interaction with his creation; specifically in his interaction with mankind?

1. God's righteousness is seen in his requiring perfect righteousness in mankind.

    Lev. 19:35-36 "You shall do no wrong in judgment, in measurement of weight, or capacity. You shall have just balances, just weights, a just ephah (bushel), and a just hin (gallon); I am the Lord your God, who brought you out from the land of Egypt." They were to live a very different life from their surrounding culture.

    Rom. 6:12-13 "Therefore do not let sin reign in your mortal body so that you obey its lusts, and do not go on presenting the members of your body to sin as instruments of unrighteousness; but present yourselves to God as those alive from the dead, and your members as instruments of righteousness to God."

2. God's righteousness is seen in his judging the unrighteous.

    Rev. 16:4-7 "The third angel poured out his bowl into the rivers and the springs of waters, and they became blood… And I heard the altar saying, 'Yes, O Lord God, the Almighty, true and righteous are Your judgments.'"

3. God's righteousness is seen in his keeping all His covenants.

    Psalm 50:5-6 "Gather My godly ones to Me, those who have made a covenant with Me by sacrifice. And the heavens declare His righteousness, for God Himself is judge."

    Ezra 9:15 "O Lord God of Israel, You are righteous, for we have been left an escaped remnant, as it is this day; behold, we are before You in our guilt, for no one can stand before You because of this."

4. God's righteousness is seen in his chastening His people.

    Daniel 9:14 "the Lord has kept the calamity in store and brought it on us; for the Lord our God is righteous with respect to all His deeds which he has done, but we have not obeyed His voice."

5. God's righteousness is clearly seen in the Cross of Christ.

    Rom. 3:25 "this (propitiation) was to demonstrate His righteousness, because in the forbearance of God He passed over the sins previously committed.

6. God's righteousness is seen in his forgiving the sins of his children.

    1 John 1:9 "If we confess our sins He is faithful and just (*sedek*) to forgive us our sins and to cleanse us from all unrighteousness."

Application of God's righteousness

In addition to how God's righteousness is seen in his interaction with mankind,

1. God's righteousness guarantees the righteous character of His Millennial Kingdom.

    Psalm 45:6 "Your throne, O God, is forever and ever; a scepter of uprightness is the scepter of Your kingdom."

2. God's righteousness guarantees the righteous nature of final judgment.

    Rev. 16:7 "I heard the altar saying, 'Yes, O Lord God, the Almighty, true and righteous are Your judgments.'"

3. God's righteousness guarantees the eternal safety of all who come to God through Christ.

    John 17:24-25a "Father, I desire that they also, whom You have given me, be with me where I am, so that they may see My glory which You have given Me, for you loved Me before the foundation of the world. O righteous Father, although the world has not known You, yet I have known You; and these have known that You sent Me."

See also John 10:27-30; Rom.8:38-39 for the security that is the believers' in Christ.

THE FAITHFULNESS OF GOD

Biblical Statement of God's Faithfulness

"Know therefore that the Lord your God, He is God, the faithful God, who keeps His covenant and His lovingkindness to a thousandth generation with those who love him and keep His commandments" (Deut. 7:9).

Both the Old Testament word and New Testament words translated "faithful" essentially mean "to be firm; reliable, steadfast, dependable, trustworthy." The Old Testament word, *aman*, in its simplest form expresses the basic concept of support (Brown-Driver-Briggs, 1980, p.52) and is used in the sense of a parent holding their infant in their arms; the baby not frightened but secure.

This idea is conveyed in Deut. 33:27a, "the eternal God is our refuge, and underneath are the everlasting arms." The Biblical emphasis of faithfulness is on the security, hope, peace that is ours because of the reliability, dependability, trustworthiness of someone else; specifically God! God's faithfulness is necessary because he cannot be anything less than faithful, and our hope for the future is intimately tied to His faithfulness.

How does the Bible describe God's faithfulness?

1. God's faithfulness is infinite; without limits.

   Psalm 36:5 "Your lovingkindness, O Lord, extends to the heavens, Your faithfulness reaches to the skies."

2. God's faithfulness is everlasting.

    Psalm 119:90 "Your faithfulness continues throughout all generations; You established the earth, and it stands."

3. God's faithfulness is an act of His will.

    Psalm 89:2 "For I have said, 'Lovingkindness will be built up forever; in the heavens You will establish Your faithfulness.'"

4. God's faithfulness is incomparable.

    Psalm 89:8 "O Lord God of hosts, who is like You, O mighty Lord? Your faithfulness also surrounds you."

5. God's faithfulness is unfailing.

    Psalm 89:33 speaking of David, "But I will not break off My lovingkindness from him, nor deal falsely in My faithfulness."

    2 Tim. 2:13 "If we are faithless, He remains faithful, for He cannot deny Himself."

6. God's faithfulness is great/majestic .

    Lam. 3:22-23 "The Lord's lovingkindness indeed never ceases, for His compassions never fail. They are new every morning; great is Your faithfulness."

In the New Testament we see references to God's faithfulness at least eleven times: 1 Cor. 1:9; 10:13; 1 Thess. 5:24; 2 Thess. 3:3; 2 Tim. 2:13; Heb. 2:7; 3:2; 10:23; 1 Peter 4:9; Rev. 1:5; 3;14.

There are hundreds of examples in Scripture that present God's faithfulness. These are only a small selection showing God's promise and His faithful fulfillment of that promise:

1. God cared for and provided for mankind after their sin in the Garden of Eden.

   God promised the Redeemer who would bring redemption to mankind (Gen. 3:15); then 4,000+ years later "we are justified freely by His grace through the Redemption that came by Christ Jesus. God presented Him as a sacrifice of atonement, through faith in His blood" (Rom. 3:24-25a).

2. God promised He would never again destroy all living creatures as He did in the Flood (Gen. 8:13, 21-22).

   For over 5,500 years God's rainbow has reaffirmed his covenant with Noah and mankind; and throughout those years He has consistently brought men, women, boys, and girls to faith in Christ!

3. God promised to deliver His people from the oppression of slavery in Egypt.

   The promise was made to Abraham (Gen. 15:13-16), and then "it came to pass at the end of the 430 years, even the self-same day it came to pass, that all the hosts of the Lord went out from the land of Egypt" (Exod. 12:41).

4. God promised to go with them in their journey to the Promised Land.

   After their sin with the golden calf and God's judgment, God said, "my presence will go with you, and I will give you rest" (Exod. 33:14). For the next 40 years, "the cloud of the Lord was over the tabernacle by day, and fire was in the cloud by night, in the sight of all the house of Israel during all their travels" (Exod. 40:37-38).

5. God promised the birth of the Messiah.

After mankind's sin in the Garden of Eden God said to the serpent, "I will put enmity between you and the woman, and between your offspring and hers; he will crush your head, and you will strike his heel" (Gen. 3:15).

Over three thousand years later he said to Isaiah, "behold, a virgin shall be with child and bear a son, and she will call His name Immanuel" (Isa. 7:14).

Seven hundred years after that, "the angel Gabriel was sent from God to a city in Galilee called Nazareth, to a virgin engaged to a man whose name was Joseph," telling her, "you have found favor with God. Behold, you will conceive in your womb and bear a son, and you shall name Him Jesus. He will be great and will be called the Son of the Most High" (Luke 1:26, 30-32).

Nine months later that promised baby was born (Luke 2:7). "When the fullness of the time came, God sent forth His Son, born of a woman, born under the Law, so that He might redeem those who were under the Law, that we might receive the adoption as sons" (Gal. 4:4-5).

What Does God's Faithfulness Mean to Us?

1. The faithfulness of God guarantees he will make good His promises and warnings; we can trust Him.

    2 Tim. 2:13 "If we are faithless, he remains faithful, for he cannot deny Himself.

    Heb. 10:23 "Let us hold fast the confession of our hope without wavering, for he who promised is faithful."

2. The faithfulness of God guarantees the continuity and stability of the world in which we live.

    Psalm 89:2 "for I have said, 'lovingkindness will be built up forever; in the heavens You will establish Your faithfulness."

    Psalm 119:90 "Your faithfulness continues throughout all generations; You established the earth, and it stands."

3. The faithfulness of God secures our participation in Christ; He will make us His children as he promised.

    1 Cor. 1:9 "God is faithful, through whom you were called into fellowship with His Son, Jesus Christ, our Lord."

4. The faithfulness of God guarantees the permanence of our salvation; we are eternally secure.

    1 Thess. 5:23-24 "Now may the God of peace Himself sanctify you entirely; and may your spirit and soul and body be preserved complete, without blame at the coming

of our Lord Jesus Christ. Faithful is He who calls you, and He also will bring it to pass."

5. The faithfulness of God guarantees our protection from the evil one: Satan.

2 Thess. 3:3 "But the Lord is faithful, and he will strengthen and protect you from the evil one."

6. The faithfulness of God secures victory for us in temptation.

1 Cor. 10:13 "No temptation has overtaken you but such as is common to man; and God is faithful, who will not allow you to be tempted beyond what you are able, but with the temptation will provide the way of escape also, so that you will be able to endure it."

7. The faithfulness of God guarantees forgiveness and cleansing of sin for believers.

1 John 1:9 "If we confess our sins, God is faithful and just to forgive us our sins, and to cleanse us from all unrighteousness."

8. The faithfulness of God enables us to trust God submissively through the most difficult experiences.

Psalm 119:75 "I know, O Lord, that Your judgments are righteous, and that in faithfulness You have afflicted me."

9. The faithfulness of God guarantees that we can believe and trust his Word.

Psalm 111:7b–8 "All His precepts are sure. They are upheld forever and ever; they are performed in truth and uprightness."

Psalm 19:7–8a "The law of the Lord is perfect, restoring the soul; the testimony of the Lord is sure, making wise the simple. The precepts of the Lord are right, rejoicing the heart."

10. The faithfulness of God guarantees that we can pray, and He will answer our prayers.

Heb. 10:21-23 "Since we have a great priest over the house of God, let us draw near with a sincere heart in full assurance of faith, having our hearts sprinkled clean from an evil conscience and our bodies washed with pure water. Let us hold fast the confession of our hope without wavering, for he who promised is faithful."

THE MERCY OF GOD

Biblical Terminology

Two Old Testament words are translated "mercy" in the Old Testament. The first is *rahum,* which is translated "mercy, tender mercy, compassion; literally "bowels" (Brown–Driver–Briggs, 1980, p.938). We see this in Psalm 111:4 "the Lord is gracious and compassionate." The second word is *hesed* and is translated "mercy, kindness, loving-kindness, goodness, pity; to stoop (Brown-Driver-Briggs, 1980, p.338). We see this in Psalm 33:5 "He loves righteousness and justice; the earth is full of the loving-kindness of the Lord."

Two New Testament Greek words are translated "mercy." The first is *oiktirmos* which is translated "mercy, merciful, tender mercy" (Bauer-Arndt-Gingrich-Danker, 1979, p.561). We see this in James 5:11 "the Lord is full of compassion and is merciful." The second is *eleos* which is translated "mercy, pity, compassion (Bauer-Arndt-Gingrich-Danker, 1979, p.250). We see this in 1 Peter 1:3 "Blessed be the God and Father of our Lord Jesus Christ, who according to His great mercy has caused us to be born again to a living hope through the resurrection of Jesus Christ from the dead."

Note the distinction between mercy and love. In general, "love" describes God's character; what He is. Mercy, on the other hand, describes God's actions; what He does! They are very different from one another. Eph. 2:4-6 gives the great distinction: "But God, being rich in mercy, because of his great love with which He loved us, even when we were dead in our transgressions, made us alive together with Christ..."

Greatness of God's Mercy

1 Chron. 21:13 "God's mercies are very great."

Psalm 57:10 "Your lovingkindness is great to the heavens."

Psalm 86:5 "You are abundant in lovingkindness to all who call upon You."

Psalm 89:2 "Lovingkindness will be built up forever; in the heavens You will establish Your faithfulness."

Psalm 108:4 "For Your lovingkindness is great above the heavens."

Psalm 119:64 "The earth is full of Your lovingkindness, O Lord."

Lam. 3:22-23 "The Lord's lovingkindnesses indeed never cease, for His compassions (mercies) never fail. They are new every morning; great is Your faithfulness."

How is God's Mercy Seen?

1. God's mercy is seen in his caring for all his creatures.

   Psalm 145:9 "the Lord is good to all, and His mercies are over all His works."

2. God's mercy is seen in His helping His people even when they do not deserve it.

   Neh. 9:17 "They refused to listen, and did not remember Your wondrous deeds which You had performed among them; so they became stubborn and appointed a leader to return to their slavery in Egypt. But You are a God of forgiveness, gracious and compassionate, slow to anger and abounding in lovingkindness; and you did not forsake them."

3. God's mercy is seen in our salvation through Christ.

   Eph. 2:4 "But God, being rich in mercy, because of his great love with which he loved us."

Practical Values of This Truth

1. It is an unmovable assurance to all who trust in God.

   Psalm 52:8 "I trust in the lovingkindness of God forever and ever.

2. It guarantees the defeat of enemies of righteousness.

   Psalm 143:12 "In lovingkindness cut off my enemies and destroy all those who afflict my soul; for I am your servant."

3. It is a great plea for us in prayer.

   Daniel 9:18 Daniel prays because of God's great compassion (mercy).

4. It demands a corresponding mercy in man.

   Luke 6:36 "Be merciful, just as your Father is merciful."

5. It is the great motive for submission to and service for God.

   Rom. 12:1 "I urge you, therefore brethren, by the mercies of God..."

6. It is the great motive for unity within the body and humility.

   Phil. 2:1-4 Put others before us.

THE JUSTICE OF GOD

Because God's righteousness and justice are translations of the same biblical word in the Old Testament, *sedek*, their meanings are determined by the subject matter of the text and the context in which it occurs. Justice is the quality of being fair. God always does what is right (from His view) as he deals with his creation. He is always fair with all of his creation.

Isa. 45:21 "Declare and set forth your case; indeed, let them consult together. Who has announced this from of old? Who has long since declared it? Is it not I, the Lord? And there is no other God beside Me, a righteous God and Savior; there is none except Me."

The interplay of these two concepts is seen in this: because God is <u>righteous,</u> He requires his children (including all mankind) to obey His laws/ His will. Because he is <u>just</u> He gives them what they deserve in relationship to their response to His laws.

<u>God's Justice Is Seen in His Upholding Righteousness (Deut. 10:17-18; Psalm 89:14)</u>

Deut. 10:17-18 "For the Lord your God is the God of gods and the Lord of lords, the great, the mighty, the awesome God who does not show partiality nor take a bribe. He executes justice for the orphan and the widow, and shows His love for the alien by giving him food and clothing."

Psalm 89:14 "Righteousness and justice are the foundation of Your throne; lovingkindness and truth go before you."

<u>God's Justice Protects the Righteous (Gen. 18:24-32; Psa. 96:11-13)</u>

Gen. 18:24-32 God said He would spare Sodom from destruction if ten righteous people were found there.

Psalm 96:11-13 "Let the heavens be glad, and let the earth rejoice; let the sea roar, and all it contains; let the field exult, and all that is in it. Then all the trees of the forest will sing for joy before the Lord, for he is coming, for he is coming to judge the earth.

He will judge the world in righteousness and the peoples in His faithfulness."

God's Justice Rewards the Righteous (Psa. 11:4-7; Matt. 5:6; 13:43; Rom. 14:10; 1 Cor. 3:12-15; 2 Cor. 5:10; 2 Tim. 4:8)

Psalm 11:4-7 "The Lord is in His holy temple; the Lord's throne is in heaven; His eyes behold, His eyelids tests the sons of men. The Lord tests the righteous and the wicked, and the one who loves violence His soul hates. Upon the wicked He will rain snares; fire and brimstone and burning wind will be the portion of their cup. For the Lord is righteous, He loves righteousness; the upright will behold His face."

2 Tim. 4:8 "In the future there is laid up for me the crown of righteousness, which the Lord, the righteous judge, will award to me on that day; and not only to me, but also to all who have loved His appearing."

2 Cor. 5:10 "For we must all appear before the judgment seat of Christ, so that each one may be recompensed for his deeds in the body, according to what he has done, whether good or bad."

God's justice punishes the wicked (Psalm 11:6; Matt. 25:46; Acts 17:31)

Psalm 11:6 "Upon the wicked He will rain snares; fire and brimstone and burning wind will be the portion of their cup."

Acts 17:31 "Because he has fixed a day in which he will judge the world in righteousness through a Man whom he has appointed, having furnished proof to all men by raising Him from the dead."

Matt. 25:46 "These will go away into eternal punishment, but the righteous into eternal life."

We see both the rewards and the punishment in Rom. 2:6-8, "God will render to each person according to his deeds: to those who by perseverance in doing good seek for glory and honor and immortality, eternal life; but to those who are selfishly ambitious and do not obey the truth but obey unrighteousness, wrath and indignation."

Justice is that which this world cries out for in every corner, in every direction. Yet, with all their crying, it will not come until Jesus returns and establishes his righteous rule upon this earth.

THE GRACE OF GOD

A short answer to the question "what is God's grace?" is that it is His unmerited favor to his children; His giving them what they do not deserve.

Biblical Texts

Gen. 6:8 "Noah found favor (grace) in the eyes of the Lord."

Jonah 4:2 "Jonah prayed to the Lord and said, 'please Lord, was not this what I said while I was still in my own country? Therefore, in order to forestall this I fled to Tarshish, for I knew that You are a gracious and compassionate God, slow to anger and abounding in lovingkindness, and one who relents concerning calamity."

Eph. 2:8 "For by grace you have been saved through faith; and that not of yourselves, it is the gift of God."

Heb. 2:9 "But we do see Him who was made for a little while lower than the angels, namely Jesus, because of the suffering of death crowned with glory and honor, so that <u>by the grace of God</u> He might taste death for everyone."

Rom. 11:5 "In the same way then, there has also come to be at the present time a remnant according to God's gracious choice."

Grace Does Not Recognize Human Merit or Works

Rom. 3:24 "Being justified as a gift by His grace through the redemption which is in Christ Jesus."

Our very best deeds are as filthy rags before our Heavenly Father. Isa. 64:6, "for all of us have become like one who is unclean, and all our righteous deeds are like a filthy garment." No matter how good we are, we cannot be good enough to merit forgiveness and eternal life with Jesus. God must deal with us in His righteousness; which shows we deserve judgment and wrath. But, because God is also gracious, He does not give us what we deserve, which is justice. He gives us what we don't deserve, which is His grace!

Grace is the Only Way God Can Save Sinners

Gal. 2:16 "Knowing that a man is not justified by the works of the Law but through faith in Christ Jesus, even we have believed in Christ Jesus, so that we may be justified by faith in Christ and not by the works of the Law; since by the works of the Law no flesh will be justified."

Paul said the same thing a little differently to Titus, "He saved us, not on the basis of deeds which we have done in righteousness, but according to His mercy, by the washing of regeneration and renewing by the Holy Spirit, whom He poured out upon us richly through Jesus Christ our Savior, so that being justified by His grace, we would be made heirs according to the hope of eternal life" (Titus 3:5-7).

Grace Keeps Us Saved

Rom. 5:1-2 "Having been justified by faith, we have peace with God through our Lord Jesus Christ, through whom also we have obtained our introduction by faith into this grace in which we stand, and we exult (rejoice) in the hope of the glory of God."

God's Grace Helps His People Obey (2 Cor. 1:12) and Persevere (2 Cor. 12:7-10) in Difficult Times

2 Cor. 1:12 "For our proud confidence is this: the testimony of our conscience, that in holiness and godly sincerity, not in fleshly wisdom but in the grace of God, we have conducted ourselves in the world, and especially toward you."

2 Cor. 12:9 Speaking of his thorn in the flesh, Paul said God gave it to keep him from becoming proud. God's words to Paul were "My grace is sufficient for you, for power is perfected in weakness."

We are saved by God's grace (Eph. 2:8); we live our Christian life in God's grace (2 Cor. 1:12; 1 Cor. 15:10; Rom. 12:3-8). God's grace is more than enough for every obstacle, problem, or circumstance that presents itself in our life (2 Cor. 9:8; 12:9-10).

Annie Johnson Flint wrote these words about God's grace:

> "He giveth more grace when the burdens grow greater,
> He sendeth more strength when the labors increase;

To added affliction He addeth His mercy,
To multiplied trials, His multiplied peace.
When we have exhausted our store of endurance,
When our strength has failed ere the day is half
done,
When we reach the end of our hoarded resources,
Our Father's full giving is only begun.
His love has no limit, His grace has no measure,
His power has no boundary known unto men;
For out of His infinite riches in Jesus,
He giveth and giveth, and giveth again!" (Flint,
1989, #351)

THE NAMES OF GOD

The question has been asked, "what is in a name?" In today's culture the selection of a name for a child born has generally little to do with family heritage, cultural background, or personal characteristics. Names may be chosen because of a favorite relative, selected from a list of names, selected from a book of names, even selected because they sound good when spoken and heard. That practice was not followed when we consider names in the Old Testament and New Testament. In these, names generally intentionally meant something; focusing upon an element of character, appearance, remembrance of some event, expressing the faith of the family, even a prophetic reference. When we look at God's names, we see God revealed through the names that he is He is called; revealing His nature, character, and works.

GOD'S NAMES IN THE OLD TESTAMENT

GOD'S PRIMARY HEBREW NAMES

Yahweh (I Am)

This is the personal name of God in the Old Testament (Jer. 33:2). It comes from the Hebrew root word "*hayah*" which means "to be, become, exist, happen" (Harris-Archer-Gleason-Waltke, 1980, 1:213). It is translated "LORD" (Psalm 110:1), JEHOVAH

(Psalm 83:18), and GOD (When following "Lord"- Gen. 15:2). It occurs approximately 6,700 times in the Old Testament. Yahweh is the living God, in contrast to all those gods who are not alive that the Egyptians and Canaanites worshipped (Jer. 10:1-16). He is the eternal unchanging God. Yahweh is God's covenant name (Gen. 15:1, 4, 18; Exod. 3:15-17; 20:1; 2 Sam. 7:4-16; Jer.31:31-37).

Elohim

This is the first descriptive term for God in the Bible. "In the beginning God (Elohim) created the heavens and the earth" (Gen.1:1). The word Elohim simply means "one who is supreme, sovereign over all." The singular forms of this name are El, Eloah, and Elah. Eloah is the poetic form and is found often in Job, and Elah is found in Ezra and Daniel. The plural form is Elohim. This name occurs approximately 2,300 times in the Old Testament, referring to the true God. This is the generic name for Deity and is translated in the King James Version as "God" (Gen. 1:1) or "gods" (Exod. 20:3). The name comes from a Hebrew root word which means "strength, might;" some theologians concluding that the general idea of this name is greatness of power. At the very least, the plural form of the word indicates plurality of persons within the Godhead. It is Elohim who enters into covenant with Abraham (Gen. 17); thus Elohim is both the Creator and Covenantal God!

Adonai

Adonai is the primary title of God in the Old Testament. It's Hebrew root form is *adon*, meaning "Lord." It is used broadly to speak of a lord of slaves (Gen. 24:29), a wife (Gen. 18:12), a people (1 Kings 22:17), a country (Gen. 42:30), a household (Gen. 45:8). Adonai, in this special plural form, always refers to God (Harris-Archer-Gleason-Waltke, 1980, 1:13); occurring in this form over 300 times in Psalms, Lamentations, and the latter prophets.

God's Compound Hebrew Names

El Shaddai- the almighty God (Gen. 17:1-2)

El Olam- the everlasting God (Gen. 21:33)

El Elyon- the Most High God (Gen. 14:18-20)

El Qodash- God, the holy one (Joshua 24:19)

El Qanno- the jealous God (Joshua 24:19)

El Elohe Israel- God, the God of Israel (Gen. 33:20)

El Roi- the God who sees (Gen. 16:13)

El Gadol waw Nora- the great and terrible God (Deut. 7:21)

El Chanun waw Rachum- the gracious and merciful God (Jonah 4:2)

El Neeman- the faithful God (Deut. 7:9)

El Chai- the living God (Joshua 3:10)

Elohim Chayim- the living God (Deut. 5:26)

Elohim Sabaoth- the God of hosts (Amos 3:13)

Yahweh Sabaoth- the LORD of hosts (1 Sam. 17:45)

Yahweh Jireh- the LORD who sees (Gen. 22:14)

Yahweh Rapha- the LORD who heals (Exod. 15:26)

Yahweh Nissi- the LORD my banner (Exod. 17:15)

Yahweh Qadash- the LORD who sanctifies (Lev. 20:8)

Yahweh Rohi- the LORD my shepherd (Psalm 23:1)

Yahweh Tsidkenu- the LORD our righteousness (Jer. 23:6)

Yahweh Shalom- the LORD is peace (Judg. 6:24)

Yahweh Shammah- the LORD is there (Ezek. 48:35)

Other Descriptive Old Testament Names

Other descriptive names for God in the Old Testament are rock (Deut. 32:4), fortress (2 Sam. 22:2), maker (Job 36:3), king (1 Sam. 12:12), Redeemer (Psalm 19:14), Savior (2 Sam. 22:3), Judge (Gen. 18:25), shield and buckler (Psalm 18:2), Glory of Israel (1 Sam. 15:29), portion (Jer. 10:16).

GOD'S NAMES IN THE NEW TESTAMENT

God (*theos*) is the generic name for deity; occurring more than 1,000 times in the New testament. It is used to refer to the Trinity (James 1:13), to the Son (1 John 5:20), to the Father (John 3:16), and to the Holy Spirit (Acts 5:3-4).

Lord (*kurios*) is the functional name for deity. It may represent either Yahweh or Adonai; depending upon their original reference in the Old Testament. Generally, it refers to God the Son (Acts 2:36; Eph. 4:5), refers to God the Father (Acts 4:24; Rev. 4:11), and on occasion refers to God the Holy Spirit (2 Cor. 3:17; Heb. 10:15-16).

There are no personal names given in the New Testament for the individual persons of the Godhead. Only their titles are presented: Father, Son, and Holy Spirit. "Jesus" is the human personal name of God the Son, and he was not given this name until after his birth.

WORKS OF GOD

CREATION

When we begin to think of the works of God, the first thing that comes to our mind is creation. The natural mind does not think of this, for man apart from God denies intelligent design, any consideration of a creator, and instead embraces chance, evolution, and even a "Big Bang."

The first thing that we hear and learn about God in Scripture is that he is the Creator. "In the beginning God created the heavens and the earth" (Gen. 1:1). If God had not told us what he did, we would have no understanding of the origin of things. We would have no guidelines for any part of life. But with a creator there must have been purpose, design, planning, and direction of how life is to operate and exist.

WHEN DID CREATION OCCUR?

"In the beginning" (Gen. 1:1); at some point in eternity past. Creation marks the beginning of time, but before creation eternity was already present. In eternity past God, the One who created all, was already there. There is no reference to time for God's presence. God the Creator is; always and forever is!

Many scientists believe the earth is billions of years old, which is a guess based on radiocarbon dating and geological data. With the operation of the James Webb telescope, they now conclude, based solely on conjecture, that they are seeing star light from 3 ½ billion years after the Big Bang. Some Christian scholars believe the earth is 10,000 years old. Recorded history begins about 3,500 years ago and prior to that one must guess. Bishop Ussher calculated and thought creation began in 4004 BC. Biblical chronological and genealogical records lead us to the Exodus (1446 BC), Abraham (2100 BC). Genesis 5-6 shows the Flood occurring about 1,656 years after creation. The available records show Ussher may not have been far off in his calculation.

WHO CREATED?

God (Elohim) created (Gen. 1:1). Creation was the work of all three persons of the Godhead. Gen. 1:1-2 tells us that God the Father was involved in creation and that the Spirit of God was moving over the waters. John 1:1-3 tells us that Jesus, God the Son-the Word, was in the beginning with God and that all things came into being through Him, and apart from Him nothing came into being that has come into being." God (Father, Son, and Holy Spirit) is always in accord with himself!

WHAT DID HE CREATE?

God didn't only create the sky above our planet, but he created "the heavens and the earth." He created the vast expanse of interstellar space and all that fills it. He created everything in the physical and spiritual realms.

Acts 4:24 "God made the heavens and the earth and the sea and everything in them."

Acts 17:24 "God made the world and everything in it."

WHY DID GOD CREATE ALL?

Over the centuries many different reasons have been proposed. Some have said that God created because He wanted fellowship. While that is a result of creation, it is not necessarily a cause. God already had fellowship within the Godhead: Father, Son, Holy Spirit. Some have said that God created the heavens and the earth to live in and have dominion over. The nature of physical creation certainly lends some credence to that possibility.

In the Biblical record of the order of creation events, the heavens and earth with its air, water, plants, birds and fish were all made during days 1-5. It was on Day 6 that God made the land animals and then said, "let Us make man in Our image" (Gen. 1:26). Did God make the world the way He did because He was going to make mankind to live in it? Or, did He make the world to fit the man He was going to make? Stated another way: was man made for the world, or was the world made for man? This is a question we will not be able to answer this side of heaven.

What we can say definitively about creation is that it was the free act of God. No outside force compelled him to do this. He did it according to the counsel of His own will (Eph. 1:11; Rev. 4:11). The primary purpose of creation seems to be to testify of his existence (Rom. 1:20; Psalm 19:1), to accomplish His purpose (Rev. 4:11; Eph. 1:11-12), and to receive praise and glory from His creatures (Psalm 148; Rev. 5:13; Rom. 11:33-36).

HOW DID GOD CREATE?

There are essentially two steps in God's work of creation. The first is that God created the universe out of nothing (*ex nihilo*);

bringing them into existence. The second part was the shaping and forming that God did; taking the elements He had made and forming them into vegetation, animal, and human life.

God, as only he could do, created everything in order. He did this in six literal 24 hour days; seen in the statement, "there was evening and there was morning, day one," etc. (Gen. 1:5). The Hebrew word for day is "*yom*." Depending upon its usage and context, it can mean a 24 hour time period; a period of light contrasted with a period of darkness; a division of time such as a working day, a day's journey; a general time; a year; a day of something (TWOT, I, P.370). Here in the days of creation account, the context states the two main components of a 24 hour day: evening and morning. This would lead to a normal conclusion that the author is referring to a 24 hour day. In addition, the use of the word "*yom*" with a numeric adjective means 24 hour days whenever this combination occurs in the Old Testament (B.K.C., I, p.28).

> Day One: He created the heavens and the earth. This included space, time, matter, energy, and all the physical laws that keep it functioning.

> Day Two: He created the earth's atmosphere.

> Day Three: He separated the sea and brought the land masses out of it. He also created vegetation.

> Day Four: He set in place the light from the sun, moon, and stars.

> Day Five: He created marine life and flying creatures; giving them a spirit.

Day Six: He created land animals, creeping forms of life, and man.

Day Seven: God rested!

GOD'S SOVEREIGN RULE

Most theologians do not consider God's sovereignty as an attribute, but they instead describe it as a prerogative of God (e.g Chafer, 1980, vol. 1, p.222). Webster defines a prerogative as "an exclusive or special right, power, or privilege; to an office or body, to a person or one possessed by a nation as an attribute of sovereignty" (Webster, Collegiate Dictionary, 10th ed., 1993, p.921). Sovereignty is further defined by the same source as "supreme power especially over a body politic; freedom from external control" (Webster, 1993, p.1125).

Sovereignty is not an attribute but is the outward expression or summation of all that God is in all His attributes. Because of all that God is (His attributes), everything must be in subservience to Him. Note these descriptions of God's sovereignty:

> Exod. 33:19 "I will be gracious to whom I will be gracious, and will show compassion whom I will show compassion."

> 1 Sam. 2:6-8 "The Lord kills and makes alive; He brings down to Sheol and raises up. The Lord makes poor and rich; He brings low, He also exalts. He raises the poor from the dust, He lifts the needy from the ash heap to make them sit with nobles, and inherit a seat of honor; for the

pillars of the earth are the Lord's, and He sets the world on them."

1 Chron. 29:11-12 "Yours, O Lord, is the greatness and the power and the glory and the victory and the majesty, indeed everything that is in the heavens and the earth; Yours is the dominion, O Lord, and You exalt Yourself as head over all. Both riches and honor come from You, and You rule over all, and in Your hand is power and might; and it lies in Your hand to make great and to strengthen everyone."

Psalm 103:19 "The Lord has established His throne in the heavens, and His sovereignty rules over all."

Psalm 115:3 "Our God is in the heavens; he does whatever He pleases."

Matt. 6:7-10 Jesus, teaching His disciples to pray said, "when you are praying, do not use meaningless repetition as the Gentiles do, for they suppose they will be heard by their many words. So, do not be like them; for your Father knows what you need before you ask Him. Pray, then in this way, 'Our Father, who is in heaven, hallowed be Your name. Your kingdom come. Your will be done, on earth as it is in heaven."

God's sovereignty is seen from the first to the last verse of Scripture: from creation to the new creation. The day is coming when God, the sovereign Lord of all, is going to bring to an end the rule of evil upon this world, establish the millennial rule of Christ, and then Himself rule all creation for eternity.

This sovereign rule of God is done through His preservation and providence.

GOD'S PRESERVATION

Here God maintains and cares for what he has made (Neh. 9:6; Col. 1:17; Heb. 1:3). He provides for needs according to His purpose for those things and creatures He has made. He cares for inanimate creation (Isa. 40:26), His creatures (Psalm 104:10-28), all people (Acts 14:17; 17:25, 28), and His elect (Psalm 37:23-29: Isa. 41:10; Matt. 6:25-34; John 6:39; 10:28).

HIS PROVIDENCE

In God's providence he directs everything to where he has determined it to go. He works out everything to accomplish His decrees. God rules natural forces (Psalm 104; Job 38:4-38) and animals (Job 38:39-39:20; 40:15-41:34). He controls the affairs of nations (Daniel 4:25; Isa. 10:5-6; 2 Chron. 10:12-16), controls individuals (Isa. 44:28; Jer. 1:5; Prov. 16:9; 20:24; 21:1), and overrules misfortune (Gen. 39:1-2, 21-23; 45:7).

DISPENSATIONS AND COVENANTS

God is working in both the Dispensations and Covenants.

DISPENSATIONS

Dispensations are essentially the responsibilities or duties that man has in his relationship with God. God is working to accomplish

His purpose in these times, and the duties mankind has vary according to the time period they are in. The Dispensations are:

Dispensation of Creation (Gen. 1-2)

Dispensation of Fallen Man-Sin (Gen. 3-4)

Dispensation of the Patriarchs (Gen. 12, 17, 26, 31, 35, 46)

Dispensation of the Mosaic Law (Exod. 20, 21-23; Lev. 1-27; Num. 5, 6, 9, 10, 27-30)

Dispensation of Grace (Titus 2:11-12; most commands of the New Testament)

Dispensation of Jesus' Rule (Isa. 2:1-3; Rev. 20:6)

COVENANTS

These are what God will do. Some of the Covenants are conditional and others unconditional.

Edenic Covenant-Conditional (Gen. 2:16-17)

Adamic Covenant- Unconditional (Gen. 3:15-17)

Noahic Covenant- Unconditional (Gen. 9:8-17)

Abrahamic Covenant- Unconditional (Gen. 17:1-19; also 12:1-3; 13:14-17; 15:4-21; 22:15-18)

Mosaic Covenant- Conditional (Exod. 19:1-8)

Palestinian Covenant- Unconditional (Deut. 28:1-29:1; 30:1-10)

Davidic Covenant- Unconditional (2 Sam. 7:10-16)

New Covenant- Unconditional (Jer. 31:31-40; Luke 22:20)

SALVATION

This is God's greatest work, because man in himself is hopelessly condemned in sin, and there is nothing he can do to help himself (Rom. 5:12). There is no one who is righteous, who deserves anything good from God (Rom. 3:10-19). The only hope for mankind was the sacrifice Jesus made to pay the redemption price for man's sin (Rom. 3:21-26). God acted in love and paid mankind's debt for his sin (John 3:16; 1 John 4:10). The death of Jesus was the ransom that gave mankind forgiveness and salvation (Matt. 20:28).

While man is to believe and receive the Son in faith (John 1:12; Rom. 10:9-10, 13), no one can do that without God choosing him (Eph. 1:4; Rev. 13:8; 17:8). We are saved by God's grace poured out to us through Jesus' death, burial, and resurrection, so that we would be declared righteous and become children of God with eternal life (Titus 3:4-7).

JUDGMENT

IN THE PAST

God is the judge of all the earth (Gen. 18:25). He has judged in the past: Adam and Eve (Gen. 3), the world of Noah's time (Gen.

6-7), Sodom and Gomorrah (Gen. 19), plagues in Egypt (Exod. 7-12), Jesus bearing our sin on the cross (Isa. 53:10; 1 John 2:2).

IN THE FUTURE

Coming judgments are during the Tribulation (Rev. 6–19), believers at the Judgment Seat of Christ (2 Cor. 5:10; Rev. 22:12), and nonbelievers at the Great White Throne (Rev. 20:11-15).

SPECIFIC WORKS OF GOD THE FATHER

Specific works are attributed to different persons of the Triune God. Those which are done by the Father only are those in our salvation and Christian walk; and those in Jesus' Messianic work.

SPECIFIC WORKS IN OUR SALVATION

He chooses who is to be saved (2 Thess. 2:13-14).

He predestines us to adoption (Eph. 1:5) and to conformity to Jesus (Rom. 8:29).

He gave Jesus to atone for our sin (1 John 4:10).

He draws us to himself (John 6:44).

He calls us to His kingdom and glory (1 Thess. 2:12).

He causes us to be born again to a living hope (1 Peter 1:3).

He keeps us safe (John 17:11-12).

He disciplines us to make us holy; to share with Him in His holiness (Heb. 12:10).

SPECIFIC WORKS IN JESUS' MESSIANIC WORK

He anointed Jesus with the Holy Spirit (John 1:32; 3:34; Phil. 2:7-8).

Jesus was doing the Father's will (John 6:38; 8:28-29).

Jesus spoke the Father's words (John 12:49-50).

Jesus was doing what his Father directed Him to do (John 5:36).

Jesus will return when His Father says "it is time" (Mark 13:32; Acts 1:7).

Jesus will be in subjection to the Father when His Millennial rule is over (1 Cor. 15:20-28).

REVIEW AND REFLECTION QUESTIONS

1. Does the Bible seek to prove the existence of God? If so, where?
2. What is the difference between these non–Christian views of God? Atheism, Agnosticism, Deism, and Theism?
3. How does God reveal Himself to mankind?
4. Name three forms of God's special revelation of himself.
5. Give biblical evidence to prove that God is a person.
6. Of what practical significance and/or value is the fact that God is a person?
7. What O.T. name for God suggests there is more than one person in the Godhead?
8. What is meant by the statement that man is made in the image of God?
9. How is Gen. 1:26; 3:22 a proof for the Trinity?
10. Name 5 attributes of God's greatness.
11. What is meant by the infinitude of God?
12. Name three things that God does not change? And why is this important in the believer's life?
13. Psalm 139 speaks of God's omniscience, omnipresence, and omnipotence. Why are these important to us in our walk with and fellowship with God?
14. Name 5 of God's attributes of goodness.
15. What are some practical values of God's holiness?
16. Describe God's love and how is that love seen in our world?
17. What do we mean by God's righteousness, and how is it seen?
18. What does God's faithfulness mean to us?
19. What is God's grace, and why is it important in the believer's life?
20. What are the 3 primary Old Testament names of God?
21. What 2 names in the New Testament refer to God?

TRIUNE GOD
- THE SON

The apostle John, as he concluded his account of the life of Christ wrote, "there are also many other things which Jesus did which if they were written in detail, I suppose that even the world itself would not contain the books that would be written" (John 21:25). As John wrote these words at the end of the 1st century A.D. there were many materials that spoke of Jesus and what he did. What was true then is even more true today. The shelves of libraries across the world are filled with tens of thousands of volumes written about the life and teachings of Jesus.

The life of the Lord Jesus Christ did not begin, as does the life of everyone else, at the moment of birth. Jesus' conception was different than the conception of every other person who has lived on earth, but his birth was the same that every other person has experienced. Jesus' conception and birth, however, were not the beginning of his existence; he came into the world from a pre-existent state to fulfil a specific mission.

PRE-EXISTENCE OF CHRIST

PRE-EXISTENCE RECORDED IN THE OLD TESTAMENT

APEARING IN THE CREATION ACCOUNT

"In the beginning God created the heavens and the earth" (Gen. 1:1). The word "God" in this verse is Elohim; the plural name for God. This includes all three persons of the triune Godhead. The Holy Spirit receives individual recognition in v.2 "the Spirit of God was moving over the surface of the waters." This becomes more clear when we read John's words in the prologue to his gospel account: "all things came into being through Him, and apart from Him nothing came into being that has come into being" (John 1:3).

APPEARING IN THE OLD TESTAMENT UNDER THE NAME JEHOVAH

The Lord (Yahweh) appeared and spoke to Abraham about Sarah's coming pregnancy and the destruction of Sodom and Gomorrah (Gen. 18). On the eve of the battle of Jericho the "captain of the host of the Lord" appeared to Joshua (Joshua 5:14-15). When Joshua saw this person and heard what was said, he fell on his face to the earth, bowed down, and worshipped. This captain of the host of the Lord did not prevent Joshua's worship but said, "remove your sandals from your feet, for the place where you are standing is holy" (v.15). Angels do not permit mankind to worship them but instead direct all worship to God. This was the pre-incarnate Christ.

Isaiah saw the Lord (Adonai) seated on his throne (Isa. 6:1-10). John 12:38-40 tells us that Isaiah saw Christ.

APPEARING IN THE OLD TESTAMENT AS THE ANGEL OF JEHOVAH

This angel appears in many Old Testament passages. He appeared and spoke to Hagar (Gen. 16:7; 21:17-18); spoke to Abraham (Gen. 22:11, 15). He spoke to Moses from the burning bush (Exod. 3:1-2), stopped Balaam's donkey to prevent Balaam from cursing the nation of Israel (Num. 22:22, 26), and spoke to Manoah and his wife about the birth of their son Samson (Judges 13).

This angel can be identified as Christ in his pre-existent state. In Judges 13:8-22 Manoah realized that this was the angel of the Lord, and he said to his wife, "we will surely die for we have seen God/Elohim (v.22). In Malachi 3:1 God, speaking with the Jews said, "behold, I am going to send My messenger, and he will clear the way before Me. And the Lord, whom you seek, will suddenly come to his temple; and the messenger of the covenant, in whom you delight, behold, He is coming." The first messenger in this text is a reference to John the Baptist. The second "messenger" is often translated "angel;" the angel of the Covenant; the Lord is the angel of the Covenant.

In Exodus 3 the angel of the Lord appeared in the burning bush to Moses (v.2), and "when the Lord saw that he turned aside to look, God called to him from the midst of the bush" (v.4), and God said, "do not come here; remove your sandals from your feet, for the place on which you are standing is holy ground" (v.5). In v.4 the Lord (Yahweh) saw and spoke. In v.6 God said, "I am the God of your father, the God of Abraham, the God of Isaac, and the God of Jacob." In v.7 "the Lord (Yahweh) said;" in v.11 Moses said to God (Elohim); in v.12 God (Elohim) said. The angel of the Lord was the one who spoke to Moses, and He is clearly identified there as God.

PRE-EXISTENCE RECORDED IN THE NEW TESTAMENT

TESTIMONY OF JOHN THE BAPTIST

John, in his testimony about Jesus said, "He who comes after me has a higher rank than I, for He existed before me" (John 1:15). John was not talking about physical birth, because he was born before Jesus. He was speaking of Jesus' pre-existence in heaven.

TESTIMONY OF JESUS HIMSELF

John 6:22-71 In the Bread of Life discourse Jesus said His Father has given them the true bread out of heaven (v.32), the bread that gives life to the world (v.33). Jesus said that He is that bread of life (v.35); "I am the living bread that came down out of heaven; if anyone eats of this bread, he will live forever; and the bread also which I will give for the life of the world is My flesh" (v.51).

John 8:42 Jesus said, "if God were your Father, you would love Me, for I proceeded forth and have come from God, for I have not even come on My own initiative, but He sent Me."

John 8:58 "Jesus said to them, 'Truly, truly, I say to you, before Abraham was born, I am.'" He was saying that he was there then, he was alive. He is God!

John 16:28-30 In the Upper Room the night of his arrest Jesus said, "I came forth from the Father and have come into the world; I am leaving the world again and going to the Father" (v.28). His disciples said, "now we know that You know all things, and have no need for anyone to question You; by this we believe that you came from God" (v.30).

John 17:5 In his prayer to His Father before going to Gethsemane Jesus said, "Now, Father, glorify Me together with Yourself, with the glory which I had with you before the world was."

TESTIMONY OF THE APOSTLES

The Apostle John

John's prologue to his gospel account clearly states the pre-existence of Christ (John 1:1-4). He began by showing Christ's pre-existence before coming into the world: "in the beginning was the Word." He showed the Son was a distinct personality from the Father: "the Word was with God." He affirmed that the Son is Deity: "the Word was God." He then stated his eternality: "he was in the beginning with God." In v.3 he shows the relationship of the Word to creation: "all things came into being through Him, and apart from him nothing came into being that has come into being."

"In Him was life, and the life was the Light of men" (v.4). The life that every creature possesses comes from the life of the One who created them. In vv.10-12 John further states that Jesus was the creator of the world and that He was incarnate, "He was in the world" (v.10). He next spoke of his reason for coming and the response to his coming (vv.10b-12). Finally, he said that the "The Word became flesh, and dwelt among us, and we saw His glory; glory as of the only begotten from the Father, full of grace and truth" (v.14).

The Apostle Paul

1 Cor. 8:6 "For us there is but one God, the Father, from whom are all things and we exist for Him; and one Lord, Jesus Christ, by whom are all things, and we exist through Him."

Eph. 1:3-5 "Blessed be the God and Father of our Lord Jesus Christ, who has blessed us with every spiritual blessing in the heavenly places in Christ, just as He chose us in Him before the foundation of the world, that we would be holy and blameless before him. In love He predestined us to adoption as sons through Jesus Christ to Himself, according to the kind intention of His will."

Phil. 2:5-7 "Have this attitude in yourselves which was also in Christ Jesus, who, although He existed in the form of God, did not regard equality with God a thing to be grasped, but emptied Himself, taking the form of a bond-servant, and being made in the likeness of men."

Col. 1:15-18 "He (Jesus) is the image of the invisible God, the firstborn of all creation. For by Him all things were created, both in the heavens and on earth, visible and invisible, whether thrones or dominions or rulers or authorities- all things have been created through Him and for Him. He is before all things, and in Him all things hold together. He is also head of the body, the church; and He is the beginning, the firstborn from the dead, so that he Himself will come to have first place in everything."

2 Tim. 1:9 "Who (God) has saved us and called us with a holy calling, not according to our works, but according to His own purpose and grace which was granted us in Christ Jesus from all eternity."

The Writer of Hebrews

Heb. 1:1-3 "God, after He spoke long ago to the fathers in the prophets in many portions and in many ways, in these last days has spoken to us in His Son, whom he appointed heir of all things, through whom He made the world. And He is the radiance of His glory and the exact representation of His nature, and upholds all things by the word of His power."

When Mary gave birth to Jesus in Bethlehem, this was not the first time he was on this earth. He has pre-existed from eternity past! Now, he was taking on human form for all of eternity; to accomplish God's will for mankind: "the Lamb of God who takes away the sin of the world."

THE INCARNATION OF CHRIST

REASON FOR THE INCARNATION

BECAUSE MANKIND SINNED (GENESIS 2:16-17; 3:1-12)

God had made a sinless world: "God saw all that he had made, and behold, it was very good" (Gen. 1:31a). God had given man a simple single command: "From any tree of the garden you may eat freely; but from the tree of the knowledge of good and evil you shall not eat, for in the day that you eat from it you will surely die" (Gen. 2:16-17). The woman was deceived by the serpent, and as she looked at the tree she "saw that it was good for food, and that it was a delight to the eyes, and that the tree was desirable to make one wise, she took from its fruit and ate" (Gen. 3:6a). "She gave also to her husband with her, and he ate" (Gen. 3:6b). The stark reality and tragic consequences that God had warned them about was immediately there. The disobedience of this first man and woman brought physical death and spiritual death upon mankind!

BECAUSE CREATION HAD NOW BEEN CURSED (GENESIS 3:13-19)

After confronting Adam and Eve with their sin, God judged every being involved in this rebellion against Him. He judged the physical serpent (v.14); He judged the spiritual serpent (v.15).

He judged the woman; what was to be a beautiful relationship and experience would now include great conflict and pain (v.16). God judged the earth (Gen. 3:17-19); now its fruitfulness would only come by extreme labor. To Adam God said, "by the sweat of your face you will eat bread, till you return to the ground, because from it you were taken; for you are dust, and to dust you shall return" (v.19). See also Rom. 8:20-22.

BECAUSE MAN NEEDED A SAVIOR

Man rejected God in the Garden of Eden and still rejects Him (Rom. 1:18-21). The evidence of God is everywhere for man to see, yet he still refuses to repent and return to God. Isaiah described our need saying, "for all of us have become like one who is unclean, and all our righteous deeds are like a filthy garment and all of us wither like a leaf, and our iniquities, like the wind, take us away" (Isa. 64:6). No one is righteous; no one seeks God. All have turned away from good and God, and every part of man's life is saturated with sin. There is no fear of God before their eyes (Rom. 3:18).

The consequences of sin continue and are all encompassing. "Therefore, just as through one man sin entered into the world, and death through sin, and so death spread to all men, because all sinned" (Rom. 5:12). Because of Adam's sin, physical and spiritual death became the grim reality for him and all his descendants. The result of that sin: "the wages of sin is death" (Rom. 6:23a).

God has the only solution to mankind's hopeless condition! Rom. 5:8 "But God demonstrates His own love toward us, in that while we were yet sinners, Christ died for us." Rom. 6:23 "For the wages of sin is death, but the free gift of God is eternal life in Christ Jesus our Lord." Rom. 10:13 "Whoever will call on the name of the Lord will be saved." Jesus himself said to his disciples the night of his arrest: "I am the Way, the Truth, and the Life. No one comes to the Father but through Me" (John 14:6).

BECAUSE GOD PROMISED A SAVIOR

Promised Before Time Began

Rev. 13:8; 17:8 speak of our names written "in the book of life of the Lamb who has been slain." Before God made anything, before creation was begun, God had already determined what He was going to do for man's forgiveness and salvation.

Promised When Mankind Sinned

God's creation was corrupted and the serpent rejoicing, but God said this was only for a period of time; when He was ready He would send the One who would defeat Satan forever (Gen. 3:15).

Promised Through A Chosen Man

God chose Abram; saying he would make of him a great nation, and all the families of the earth would be blessed through him (Gen. 12:1-3). From this man would come the Savior; Matt. 1 and Luke 3 genealogies.

Promised A Savior/Messiah Who would Be Prophet And King

He is the prophet who was to come: the Messiah (Deut. 18:15). God's Holy Spirit is upon him (Isa. 11:2). He will be a righteous judge who brings righteousness and justice (Psalm 72:2). He will be ruler of Israel, King of the Jews (Gen. 49:10; Jer. 23:5-6). He will be born of a virgin (Isa. 7:14) and born in Bethlehem (Micah 5:2). He will be recognized by how he presents himself (Zech. 9:9). His will be an eternal righteous reign on David's throne (Isa.

9:6-7). He is exalted and at God's right hand until all his enemies are submitted to him (Isa. 52:13; Psalm 110:1).

Promised A Savior/Messiah Who Would Be The Suffering Servant

Isa. 42:1-4 "Behold, My Servant, whom I uphold; My chosen one in whom My soul delights..."

Isa. 52:13-53:12 His work as the suffering servant is described.

BECAUSE GOD KEEPS HIS PROMISES

1 Thess. 5:24 "Faithful is he who calls you, and he also will bring it to pass." What God has promised, He will do! He promised a Savior, and Jesus came as the fulfillment of those promises.

We have already seen that God's faithfulness is without limits (Psalm 36:5) and unfailing (Psalm 89:33). Because of that we can always trust His word (Psalm 119:138); what he says he will do, he will do! Therefore, "when the fullness of the time came, God sent forth His son, born of a woman, born under the Law, so that He might redeem those who were under the Law, that we might receive the adoption as sons" (Gal. 4:4-5).

FACT OF THE INCARNATION

Approximately 700 BC Micah prophesied to the people of Judah, "but as for you, Bethlehem Ephrathah, too little to be among the clans of Judah, from you One will go forth for Me to be ruler in Israel. His goings forth are from long ago, from the days of eternity. Therefore He will give them up until the time when she who is in labor has borne a child. Then the remainder of His brethren will return to the sons of Israel" (Micah 5:2-3).

Israel had already been taken captive by the Assyrians and Judah was in great danger of suffering the same captivity. The answer to Judah's looming danger was not in military power but in the One whom God would send to provide deliverance for His people. As Micah describes what God is going to do, he speaks of Jesus' first coming (vv.2-3) and then of his second coming (vv.4-15).

Micah's words in vv.2-3 point the reader to the Incarnation, for the One who is coming is not simply going to be born in Bethlehem, as every other baby has been born. This One has been living from long ago, from the days of eternity (v.2). These words speak of the pre-existence of Jesus. It was not yet time for the Messiah to be born, but 700 years later it will be time. "When the fullness of the time came, God sent forth His Son, born of a woman, born under the Law, so that he might redeem those who were under the Law" (Gal. 4:4-5). Micah said God would send him forth, and Paul said that God had sent Him forth!

Incarnation is that act of God by which the second person of the Triune God is embodied in human nature, flesh, and form. There were several pre-incarnate appearances of Christ noted throughout the Old Testament, but those were brief, temporary appearances to accomplish a specific purpose. The incarnation of Jesus was very different. It was not temporary but permanent; taking on human flesh and form forever.

The key statement of Christ's incarnation is found in John's prologue to his Gospel account. After stating that Jesus is God (vv.1-5) he said, "and the Word became flesh, and dwelt among us, and we saw His glory, glory as of the only begotten from the Father, full of grace and truth" (John 1:14). God took upon Himself human flesh and dwelt with mankind, and in Him John and others saw God's glory.

Belief in and proclamation of the incarnation is one of the tests of truth and error, determining true teachers from false teachers. "By this you know the Spirit of God: every spirit that confesses that Jesus Christ has come in the flesh is from God; and every spirit that does not confess Jesus is not from God; this is the spirit of the antichrist" (1 John 4:2-3a).

BIBLICAL EXPRESSIONS OF JESUS' INCARNATION

Stating that a baby has been born was easy to do: Elizabeth became pregnant (Luke 1:24), and when it was time she gave birth to a son (Luke 1:57). Because Christ had pre-existed from all eternity, to state that the second person of the Godhead had permanently come into human flesh and form was much more difficult to do. Luke's description of Jesus' birth is very simple: "she gave birth to her firstborn son" (Luke 2:7a), but other New Testament writers chose very different words to describe this very different conception and birth.

> Matt. 20:28 Speaking of himself Jesus said, "the Son of Man did not come to be served, but to serve, and to give His life a ransom for many."

> John 3:13 "No one has ascended into heaven, but He who descended from heaven: the Son of Man."

> John 3:17 "For God did not send the Son into the world to judge the world, but that the world might be saved through Him."

> John 6:51 "I am the living bread that came down out of heaven..."

Rom. 8:3 "For what the Law could not do, weak as it was through the flesh, God did: <u>sending His Son</u> in the likeness of sinful flesh..."

Phil. 2:7 He "emptied Himself, taking the form of a bond-servant, and being <u>made in the likeness of men</u>."

These additional verses further show the difficulty the Scripture writers had as they sought to describe what God had done in the incarnation of Jesus: 1 Tim. 1:15; 3:16; Heb. 2:14, 17; 10:5; 1 John 3:5.

CHANGES FOR THE SECOND PERSON OF THE GODHEAD IN THE INCARNATION (Whitcomb, 1982, pp. 27-28)

<u>Change in His Dwelling Place: From Heaven to Earth</u>

While He came to earth for his pre-incarnate appearances, Jesus' dwelling place for all eternity had been heaven. Now his dwelling place would be earth! Jesus said to the Jews, "I am the living bread that came down out of heaven..." (John 6:51).

<u>Change in His Possessions: From Riches to Poverty</u>

Jesus said to His disciples, "the foxes have holes and the birds of the air have nests, but the Son of Man has nowhere to lay His head" (Luke 9:58).

2 Cor. 8:9 "For you know the grace of our Lord Jesus Christ, that though he was rich, yet for your sake He became poor, so that you through His poverty might become rich."

Change in His Glory: From Glory to Obscurity

John 1:10 "He was in the world, and the world was made through Him, and the world did not know Him."

John 17:5 "Now, Father, glorify Me together with Yourself, with the glory which I had with You before the world was."

Change in His Position: From Equality with God to Servanthood

Matt. 20:28 "The Son of Man did not come to be served, but to serve, and to give his life a ransom for many."

Phil. 2:6-7 "Who, although He existed in the form of God did not regard equality with God a thing to be grasped, but emptied Himself, taking the form of a bond-servant, and being made in the likeness of men."

Change in His form: From the Form of God to the Likeness of Men

All of the other changes that occurred were temporary, but this one was permanent. When Jesus ascended to heaven, he received back all He had left behind, was clothed again with His glory as God, and was again seated on the throne of the universe. Yet now, He sits there as God, in human form.

Acts 1:8 When Jesus ascended into heaven he did so in bodily form.

Acts 7:54-56 Stephen said he saw the Son of Man standing on the right hand of God.

Rev. 1:13, 17-18 John saw one like a son of man (v.13), and the One he saw "placed His right hand on him, saying, 'do not be afraid; I am the first and the last, and the living One; and I was dead, and behold, I am alive forevermore...'"

Rev. 22:16 "I, Jesus, have sent My angel to testify to you these things for the churches, I am the root and the descendant of David, the bright morning star."

There was no change for Jesus in His Divine Personality. When he became man he did not cease to be God. When he received back the glory of God he did not cease to be man. Through all of the changes of position, form, and state Jesus remained the same person: "Jesus Christ is the same yesterday and today and forever" (Heb. 13:8).

VIRGIN BIRTH

When the angel Gabriel came to Mary, he announced that she was going to conceive and bear a son whom she was to name Jesus. He would be called the Son of the Most High, would sit on the throne of His father David, and will reign over the house of Jacob, and His kingdom will never end (Luke 1:30-33). Mary had only one question for Gabriel: "how can this be, since I am a virgin?" (v.34). Gabriel's answer was, "the Holy Spirit will come upon you, and the power of the Most High will overshadow you; and for that reason the holy Child shall be called the Son of God" (v.35).

Mary was not just a young woman as some have inaccurately translated and interpreted the passage; she was a virgin. What she had just been told was humanly impossible apart from the normal means of procreation. It could only happen as God intervened and caused it, which is exactly what Gabriel said would occur and did occur. All three persons of the Godhead were involved in creation, and one of those involved in making Mary's body, the Holy Spirit, would supernaturally touch her body and cause her to be pregnant. Her response: "behold, the bond-slave of the Lord; may it be done to me according to your word" (v.38). This miracle of God, through which the Son of God came into this world, was a virgin conception and virgin birth.

VIRGIN BIRTH IN THE OLD TESTAMENT

In Gen. 3:15 God said in judgment upon the serpent, "I will put enmity between you and the woman, and between your seed and her seed; He shall bruise you on the head, and you shall bruise him on the heel." To Noah (Gen. 9:9), Abram (Gen. 12:7; 13:15; 15:5), Lot's daughters (Gen. 19:32), Isaac (Gen. 26:4, 24) we see the reference to the seed of the man. Here in Gen. 3:15 the reference is specifically to the seed of the woman.

In Isa. 7:14 God said to King Ahaz to ask for a sign that Judah would be delivered from her enemies. When Ahaz refused, God said He himself would give him a sign: "behold a virgin will be with child and bear a son, and she will call His name Immanuel." While the Hebrew word "*almah*" translated virgin, can mean "young woman, virgin," the Septuagint translation of the Hebrew text uses the Greek word *parthenos* to describe her. *Parthenos* is a technical Greek word for virgin (Bauer-Arndt-Gingrich-Danker, 1979, p.627).

VIRGIN BIRTH IN THE NEW TESTAMENT

Matt. 1:18-25 The angel told Joseph that Mary had not been unfaithful; "the Child who has been conceived in her is of the Holy Spirit" (v.20b). He also told him that what has taken place is to fulfill what God had spoken through the prophet Isaiah (Isa. 7:14). Joseph immediately took Mary into his home as his wife, and he kept her a virgin until she had given birth to Jesus (vv.24-25).

Luke 1:26-38 When told that she was going to conceive and give birth to a son who would be named Jesus, who would be the Son of the Most High, who would rule over Jacob's house and have an eternal kingdom, she asked how this could occur because she was a virgin. She was told that God would do this through her.

Matt. 1:16 This is Jesus' genealogy through his step-father Joseph. All the other references in the list state "the father of," but here the writer specifically states, "Mary, by whom Jesus was born." While the genealogy shows his legal right to the throne of David through Solomon, the writer is intentionally showing that the birth was different than all the others. The birth through all the others was tied to the father, but here the birth was specifically attributed to the mother alone.

Luke 3:23-37 This is Jesus' genealogy through his mother Mary. This genealogy establishes the bloodline right to the throne of David. V.23 indicates that Jesus was "supposed" the son of Joseph, the son of Eli. This genealogical list is that of Mary, through Nathan to David, to Adam. Both Matthew's and Luke's genealogies establish Jesus' right to the throne of David, and both establish that Joseph was not the father of Jesus!

Mark 1:11 When Jesus was baptized God spoke from heaven saying, "You are My beloved Son, in You I am well-pleased."

John 1:14 "And the Word became flesh, and dwelt among us, and we saw His glory, glory as of the only begotten from the Father, full of grace and truth."

Luke 2:48-49 At age 12 in the temple Jesus said to his mother Mary, "why is that you were looking for Me? Did you not know that I had to be in My Father's house?"

The apostle Paul wote in Rom. 1:3 "concerning His Son, who was born of a descendant of David according to the flesh." We also see Gal. 4:4 where he stated, "God sent forth His son, born of a woman, born under the Law."

Some indirect evidences of the Virgin Birth are:

Matt. 2:11, 13 The magi "saw the Child with Mary His mother... After the magi left the angel told Joseph "take the child and His mother and flee to Egypt". There is no reference to Joseph being the child's father.

Luke 2:26 The Holy Spirit had revealed to Simeon that he would not see death before he had seen the Lord's Christ. The Christ (Messiah) to come will be born of a virgin (Isa.7:14). Jesus is the fulfillment of that prophecy.

IMPORTANCE OF THE VIRGIN BIRTH

The virgin birth is essential to the truth of the gospel records. If Matthew and Luke were wrong about the virgin birth, then how can we trust anything else that they have written?

The virgin birth is essential to our Lord's sinless nature. Jesus was fully man, born of a human mother. He was already deity, and through Mary he gained humanity; possessing a human nature. He was one person with two natures: Divine and Human. The union and relationship of these two natures in Jesus is called the hypostatic union.

The virgin birth is necessary to solve the problem of Jeremiah's curse on Solomon's line (Jer. 22:30).

The virgin birth protects Jesus and Mary from the accusations of illegitimacy that would have reached far beyond his physical life but also down through the ensuing centuries.

HUMANITY OF CHRIST

Jesus did not simply appear human, but he was genuinely truly human in every aspect except one: sinfulness.

SCRIPTURE PRESENTS HIM AS HUMAN

He is called by names that imply that he has a human nature. He is called "the man Christ Jesus" (1 Tim. 2:5), Son of Man (John 5:27), son of Mary (Mark 6:3), a baby (Luke 2:12), a boy (Luke 2:43). He said he was a man (John 8:40).

These additional Scriptures speak of his humanness: Heb. 2:14 "partaker of flesh and blood;" Rom. 1:3 "born as a descendant of David according to the flesh;" Acts 2:30 "a descendant of David."

CHRIST DISPLAYED ALL THE APPEARANCES OF HUMANNESS

He had prenatal development and birth as every other person (Luke 2:5-7). He had human appearance (John 4:9; 8:57: 10:33) and grew and developed as every other child (Luke 2:40, 52). He displayed the emotions that are commonly found in people: sorrow and grief (Isa. 53:5; Mark 3:5), concern (John 13:21), sorrow (John 11:35), joy (Luke 10:21), anger (Mark 3:5), love (John 13:23).

Jesus had normal human appetites and limitations. He was hungry (Matt. 4:2), thirsty (John 19:28), was weary (John 4:6), needed sleep (Matt. 8:24), needed strengthening (Luke 22:43), learned obedience (Heb. 5:8). He experienced temptation as all people do, but He did not sin (Heb. 4:15). He died as every person dies (John 19:30, 34; Heb. 2:9, 14).

CHRIST'S HUMANITY WAS PERFECT AND SINLESS

"Just as through one man sin entered into the world, and death through sin, and so death spread to all men, because all sinned" (Rom. 5:12). When people looked at Jesus, they were looking at God in the flesh. The apostle John said, "we saw His glory, glory as of the only begotten from the Father, full of grace and truth" (John 1:14).

One commentator described Christ, "He embraces all the good elements which mark other men...He possesses all these in a higher degree than any one else, and with perfect balance and proportion. There is no weakness, no exaggeration or strain, no strong or weak points, as is the case with the rest of mankind. There are certain elements and traits of character which are not found elsewhere, such as absolute humility, entire unselfishness, whole-hearted willingness to forgive, and perfect holiness" (W. H. Griffith Thomas, 1916, p.12).

Jesus never sinned, nor was he a sinner. He never confessed sin and never sought forgiveness. He submitted to John's baptism, but it was not for repentance but for the anointing of the Holy Spirit as He began His ministry (John 1:32).

WRONG THEORIES OF CHRIST'S HUMANITY

Docetism (Unreal Humanity)

This theory came from Serapion of Antioch (A.D. 197-203). This is a gnostic philosophy that says that matter is evil. Because God is infinite he could not be contaminated by material physical substance; therefore He could not be incarnate. This position states that Jesus only had the appearance of material human flesh. An offshoot of this view states that Jesus was a true human child born to Joseph and Mary, and that it was at his baptism that Christ came upon him. A modern day form of this is Christian Science.

Apollinarianism (Incomplete Humanity)

The founder of this view, Apollinaris of Laodicea, who died A.D. 390, divided man into body, irrational soul, and rational soul (intellect). He stated that in the incarnation the rational soul (intellect) of the man Christ Jesus was replaced by the eternal spirit of the Logos. Essentially he was saying that Jesus did not have a human mind. In this view only the body is redeemed, not the heart, the mind.

DEITY OF CHRIST

Throughout His ministry Jesus said that he was God, that He was the Son of God. To the woman at the well in Samaria who said she knew the Messiah, who is called Christ, is coming, Jesus said, "I who speak to you am He" (John 4:26). To the Jews in the temple who were accusing Jesus of being possessed by a demon Jesus said, "My Father, whom you say is your God, glorifies me... Abraham rejoiced to see my day" (John 8:54-56). When they disputed with him, Jesus said, "truly I say to you, before Abraham was born, I am" (John 8:58). Because of that they were going to stone him to death for blasphemy. Walking in the temple at the Feast of Dedication, Jesus said to the Jewish leaders there, "I and the Father are one" (John 10:30), and they were going to stone him to death then for blasphemy.

After his arrest in the Garden of Gethsemane Jesus was taken to stand trial before Annas, Caiaphas, and then before the Sanhedrin. As he stood before the Sanhedrin they said, "if You are the Christ, tell us," and Jesus said to them, "if I tell you, you won't believe, and if I ask a question, you won't answer. But from now on the Son of Man will be seated at the right hand of the power of God" (Luke 22:67-69). Then they asked him directly, "are You the Son of God, then?" (v.70); to which Jesus answered, "Yes, I am" (v.70). While they brought other charges against him in the trials before Pilate, this was the primary one: "we have a law, and by that law

He ought to die because He made Himself out to be the Son of God" (John 19:7).

The night of his arrest Jesus said to his disciples, "I am the Way, the Truth, and the Life; no one comes to the Father but through Me" (John 14:6). He alone is the Way to forgiveness and heaven; he alone gives Life, eternal life, to those who come to him in faith believing. He alone is the Truth; Jesus said I am the Messiah, the Christ; I am God; I am the Son of God!

NAMES GIVEN TO HIM WHICH CAN ONLY BE APPLIED TO GOD

HE IS CALLED GOD

John 1:1 "In the beginning was the Word, and the Word was with God, and the Word was God."

John 1:18 "No one has seen God at any time; the only begotten God who is in the bosom of the Father, He has explained Him."

John 20:28 Thomas said to Jesus, "my Lord and my God."

Titus 2:13 "Looking for the blessed hope and the appearing of the glory of our great God and Savior, Christ Jesus."

Heb. 1:8 "But of the Son he says, 'Your throne, O God, is forever and ever, and the righteous scepter is the scepter of His kingdom.'"

1 John 5:20 "And we know that the Son of God has come, and has given us understanding so that we may know Him who is true; and we are in Him who is true, in His Son Jesus Christ. This is the true God and eternal life."

HE IS CALLED THE SON OF GOD

Luke 1:35 Gabriel said to Mary, "the holy Child shall be called the Son of God."

John 1:34 John the Baptist said of Jesus, "I myself have seen, and have testified that this is the Son of God."

John 10:36 Jesus said, "I am the Son of God."

The word "son" (Greek *huios*) refers to position in the relationship, not origin. The Greek word for child, *teknon,* refers to origin. As Jesus referred to himself as the Son (Greek *huios*), he was saying that he was equal with God. Those who were condemning Him knew exactly what Jesus was saying. They knew that Jesus was not saying he was made by God, but knew He was stating he was God by position: equal with God.

When Jesus referred to himself as the Son of Man he was also referring to position and not origin. Jesus' origin was not of man; though born through Mary his origin was through the Holy Spirit. As Son of Man he was stating his position, His true humanity. As Son of God he was stating his position, His true deity!

HE IS CALLED LORD

The Hebrew Old Testament was translated into Greek about 250 years before the birth of Jesus. In that translation the name *Jehovah* was translated as the Greek word *kurios*. Jesus is called Lord (*kurios*) in Luke 2:11; John 13:13; Rom. 10:9; 1 Cor. 12:3; Phil. 2:10, and many other passages.

HE IS CALLED THE LORD OF GLORY

In Psalm 24:8-10 the Lord (Jehovah) is called the King of glory. In 1 Cor. 2:8 Jesus is called the Lord (*Kurios*) of glory.

HE IS CALLED THE HOLY ONE

Isa. 48:17 "Thus says the Lord, your Redeemer, the Holy One of Israel;" and Hosea 11:9 "For I am God and not man, the Holy One in your midst." Peter preaching in the temple referring to Jesus said to the crowd, "you disowned the Holy and Righteous One and asked for a murderer to be granted to you" (Acts 3:14).

HE IS CALL THE FIRST AND THE LAST; THE ALPHA AND OMEGA

God is called the first and last in Isa. 44:6; 48:12-16, and Jesus is called the first and the last in Rev. 1:17-18; 22:13, 16.

ATRIBUTES ARE HIS THAT CAN ONLY BELONG TO GOD

While the attributes of God have been previously discussed in great detail, these will be restated with specific reference to Jesus. In Jesus <u>all</u> the fullness of the Godhead dwells bodily (Col. 2:9).

ATTRIBUTES OF GREATNESS

Christ Has Self-Existent Life

John 1:4 "In Him was life, and the life was the Light of men."

John 5:26 "For just as the Father has life in Himself, even so He gave to the Son also to have life in Himself.'

John 14:6 Jesus said, "I am the way, the truth, and the life…"

Christ is Eternal

John 8:35-36 "The Son remains forever. So if the Son makes you free, you will be free indeed."

1 John 5:11 "And the testimony is this, that God has given us eternal life, and this life is in His Son."

Christ is Unchangeable

Heb. 1: 10-12 "You, Lord, in the beginning laid the foundation of the earth, and the heavens are the works of Your hands; they will perish, but You remain; and they will become old like a garment, and like a mantle You will roll them up; like a garment they will also be changed. But You are the same, and Your years will not come to an end."

Heb. 13:8 "Jesus Christ is the same yesterday and today and forever."

Christ is Omnipresent

Matt. 18:20 "For where two or three have gathered together in My name, I am there in their midst."

Matt. 28:20 "Lo, I am with you always, even to the end of the age."

Christ is Omniscient

During his Incarnation Jesus knew all men and what was in mankind (John 2:24-25; see also Jer. 17:9-10). Examples of his omniscience are Matt. 17:24-27; Luke 5:22; John 1:48; 4:16-19; 21:6.

At the same time there were some things that he was being taught by His Father, and times that He was speaking what His Father had told him to say. The apostle Paul said that when Jesus came to earth he voluntarily emptied himself (Phil. 2:5-7). While he never gave up any of his attributes, he did put restrictions upon his independent usage of some of them. As God he could always know everything, but as man there were times when he could not know without divine revelation.

After Jesus' ascension to heaven Paul tells us that all the treasures of wisdom are hidden in him (Col. 2:3). The letters to the seven church show Jesus' knowledge (Rev. 2:2, 9, 13; 3:1, 8, 15).

Christ is Omnipotent

During his earthly ministry Jesus cured illnesses (Luke 4:39), controlled nature (Matt. 8:26-27), cast out demons (Mark 5:12-13), raised the dead (Luke 7:14-15).

Since His ascension into heaven he is able to subject all things to himself (Phil. 3:20-21) and is coming back to judge and rule (Rev. 22:12-13, 16).

Christ is Perfect

Col. 2:9-10 "In Him all the fullness of Deity dwells in bodily form, and in Him you have been made complete..."

Christ is Infinite

John 10:28 "I will give eternal life to them, and they will never perish; and no one will snatch them out of my hand."

Col. 2:3 "In Him are hidden all the treasures of wisdom and knowledge."

Christ is Incomprehensible

Matt 11:27 "No one knows the Son except the father; nor does anyone know the Father except the Son."

Eph. 3:8 "the unfathomable riches of Christ."

Eph. 3:19 "the love of Christ which surpasses knowledge."

ATTRIBUTES OF GOODNESS

Christ is Holy

Luke 1:35 The Holy child

Acts 3:14 "the holy and righteous One"

Christ is True

John 14:6 Jesus said, "I am the truth..."

Christ is Love

Rom. 8:35–39 Nothing can separate us from Christ's love.

1 John 3:16 "We know love by this, that He laid down His life for us."

Christ is Righteous

2 Tim. 4:8 "The Lord, the righteous judge."

1 John 2:1 Our advocate, "Jesus Christ the righteous."

Christ is Faithful

Rev. 3:14 He is the "faithful and true Witness."

Rev. 19:11 The Lord on the white horse is called "Faithful and True."

Christ is Merciful

Jude 21 "Keep yourselves in the love of God, waiting anxiously for the mercy of our Lord Jesus Christ to eternal life."

WORKS ARE DONE BY CHRIST THAT ONLY GOD CAN DO

Some of these have already been discussed earlier in The Works of God, of the Godhead.

CREATION

Along with the other members of the Godhead, Jesus, the Son of God created all things (Gen 1:1; John 1:3; Col. 1;16).

UPHOLDING/SUSTAINING ALL THINGS

"He is before all things, and in Him all things hold together" (Col. 1:17). He keeps everything together so that it does not fall apart and disintegrate into a million different directions. Said another way, He keeps the natural laws working through which the universe and this earth are held together and continue functioning.

"He upholds all things by the word of His power" (Heb. 1:3b). Just as God spoke and creation occurred, the continuance of creation is there by the spoken word of God the Son. The sun continues to shine, because God the Son says it is to continue to shine. The sun follows its daily course, because God the Son said it is to continue (Psalm 19:4-6). Lazarus came back from the dead as Jesus stood at his tomb and said, "Lazarus, come forth" (John 11:43).

GUIDES AND DIRECTS HISTORY

Guided Israel in the Wilderness

1 Cor. 10:4, 9, 11 "All drank the same spiritual drink, for they were drinking from a spiritual rock which followed them; and the rock was Christ...nor let us try the Lord, as some of them did, and were destroyed by the serpents… now these things happened to them as an example, and they were written for our instruction, upon whom the ends of the ages have come."

Opens the Seven Seals on the Scroll

Jesus will take the scroll out of the hand of His Father, who is seated on the throne in heaven (Rev. 5:7), and as he does so, the elders and the four living creatures fall down in worship before him and sing this song: "worthy are You to take the book and to break its seals; for You were slain, and purchased for God with Your blood men from every tribe and tongue and people and nation" (Rev. 5:9). One-by-one Jesus opens the scrolls (Rev. 5:5; 6:1, 3, 5, 7, 9, 12; 8:1); directing every phase of the Tribulation.

FORGIVES SINS AND GIVES ETERNAL LIFE

Isa. 43:25 "I, even I, am the one who wipes out your transgressions for My own sake, and I will not remember your sins." To the paralytic in Capernaum Jesus said, "Son, your sins are forgiven;"

then he told him to pick up his pallet and go home (Mark 2:5-11). To the crowd in the temple during the Feast of Dedication Jesus said, "My sheep hear My voice, and I know them, and they follow Me; and I give eternal life to them, and they will never perish" (John 10:27-28a).

BUILDS THE CHURCH

Near Caesarea Philippi Jesus said to His disciples, "upon this rock I will build My church; and the gates of Hades will not overpower it" (Matt. 16:18).

RECEIVES AND ANSWERS PRAYER

John 14:13-14 "Whatever you ask in My name, that will I do, so that the Father may be glorified in the Son. If you ask Me anything in My name, I will do it." While we can pray to each member of the Godhead, Jesus said here that we can ask in His name.

ADMINISTERS FINAL JUDGMENT UPON THE WORLD

Matt. 25:31-46 shows the judgment that will come upon all mankind when Jesus returns to set up His kingdom. He will be the judge before whom all will stand. "When the Son of Man comes in His glory, and all the angels with Him, then He will sit on His glorious throne. All the nations will be gathered before Him; and he will separate them from one another, as the shepherd separates the sheep from the goats (vv.31-32)... To some He will say, 'come, you who are blessed of My Father, inherit the kingdom prepared for you from the foundation of the world' (v.34)...to others, 'depart from Me, accursed ones, into the eternal fire which has been prepared for the devil and his angels'"(v.41).

John 5:22 "Not even the Father judges anyone, but he has given all judgment to the Son."

WORSHIP IS GIVEN TO CHRIST
WHICH BELONGS ONLY TO GOD

When Jesus was tempted at the beginning of His ministry by Satan, Satan said he would give Him all the kingdoms of the world, if He (Jesus) would fall down and worship him (Matt. 4:8-9). Jesus' answer to this temptation was "Go, Satan! For it is written, 'you shall worship the Lord your God, and serve Him only'" (v.10). Jesus was quoting Deuteronomy 6:13-15.

CHRIST ACCEPTED AND ENCOURAGED
WORSHIPPING HIM

Matt. 14:31-33 The disciples worshipped Jesus after He saved Peter and the severe storm stopped.

Matt. 15:25-28 The Syro-Phoenician woman worshipped Jesus.

Matt. 28:9-10 When Jesus met the women who had just left the empty tomb, they "took hold of his feet and worshipped him."

Matt. 28:16-18 After His resurrection, when the disciples met Jesus in Galilee they worshipped him.

CHRIST DEMANDED WORSHIP

John 5:23 all judgment is given to the Son "so that all will honor the Son even as they honor the Father. He who does not honor the Son does not honor the Father who sent Him."

GOD COMMANDS WORSHP OF CHRIST

Heb. 1:6 "And when he again brings the firstborn into the world, He says, "and let all the angels of God worship Him."

HOST OF HEAVEN WILL WORSHIP CHRIST

Rev. 5:8 the living creatures and the elders will fall down before the Lamb.

ALL LIVING CREATION WILL WORSHIP CHRIST

Phil. 2:10-11 "At the name of Jesus every knee will bow, of those who are in heaven and on earth and under the earth, and that every tongue will confess that Jesus Christ is Lord, to the glory of God the Father."

CLAIMS MADE BY CHRIST THAT COULD ONLY BE TRUE BY ONE WHO IS GOD

CLAIMED ABSOLUTE AUTHORITY OVER THE LAWS AND INSTITUTIONS OF GOD

He claimed authority over the Law of Moses (Matt. 5:31-34). He said he was greater than the temple (Matt. 12:6). He said He was Lord of the Sabbath (Matt. 12:8). He said He has the keys to the kingdom (Matt. 16:19).

CLAIMED EQUALITY WITH THE FATHER IN SALVATION

He said that He and His Father are one (John 10:30); you believe in God, believe also in Me (John 14:1). He prayed, "this is eternal life, that they may know You, the only true God, and Jesus Christ whom You have sent" (John 17:3).

CLAIMED TO BE THE TRUE OBJECT OF MEN'S FAITH AND DEVOTION

Follow Me (Matt. 4:19); come to Me (Matt. 11:28); believe in the Son (John 3:36). To Peter, "do you love me... tend My lambs... shepherd My sheep... tend My sheep" (John 21:15-17).

CLAIMED HE SATISFIES MANKIND'S DEEPEST AND ETERNAL NEEDS

Knowledge of God comes through Him (Matt. 11:27); He is the only way to God (John 14:6); He is the door to salvation (John 10:7-9); He is light for the soul (John 8:12). He is the bread of life (John 6:35, 51); He is rest for the soul (Matt. 11:28-29); He gives eternal life (John 10:28-30); He is the resurrection and life (John 11:25-26).

WITNESS OF OTHERS TO DEITY OF CHRIST

Witness of God the Father (John 5:17-18, 31-39), witness of John the Baptist (John 1:34; 3:31); witness of Nathanael (John 1:49); Peter (Matt. 16:16-17); John the apostle (John 20:30-31; 1 John 5:20). Additionally, the centurion (Mark 5:39), Satan (Matt. 4:3, 6- the "if" here refers to certainty), and demons (Mark 1:24) are witnesses to the Deity of Christ.

PERSON OF CHRIST

Jesus, from eternity past, has always existed; possessing the divine nature. Through His conception in Mary's body and subsequent birth He took upon himself a human nature. From conception on Jesus had both a divine nature and a human nature. The union of these two natures, human and divine in one person is called the "hypostatic union." "Hypostatic" is from the Greek word *hupostasis*, meaning "that which comes under" (Bauer-Arndt-Gingrich-Danker, 1979, p.847). Jesus is not two persons, one human and one divine but one person with two natures; making Him the God-man.

The many acts, powers, and attributes of the two natures are ascribed to one person, not two. In Luke 1:31-33 we see his name will be Jesus (human); he will be the son of the Most High (divine). In Acts 20:28 we see "be on guard for yourselves and for all the flock, among which the Holy Spirit made you overseers, to shepherd the church of God (divine) which He purchased with his own blood (human)."

There is no interaction or exchange between the two natures; no mixing or combining to form a new nature. There was no conflict or competition between the two natures; but always working in complete cooperation with one another. When Jesus slept in the boat in the middle of the storm (Matt. 8:24), he was still God, and when they awakened Him he "rebuked the winds and the sea, and it became perfectly calm" (v.26).

Paul wrote of Jesus' human nature, "Jesus, who although He existed in the form of God (divine nature), did not regard equality with God a thing to be grasped, but emptied Himself, taking the form of a bond-servant, and being made in the likeness of men (Phil. 2:5-7). Jesus did not give up any part of his divine nature or divine attributes, but He voluntarily put them in submission to his human nature. Thus, He was God when the crowd came to arrest him in Gethsemane, and He could have called twelve legions of angels to come to his rescue (Matt. 26:53), but as man he was arrested and taken away. Throughout his life on earth Jesus' divine nature was "under," in submission to his human nature; always to accomplish God's will.

This union of the human and divine natures in Jesus, made it possible for one person to be the Mediator between God and man (1 Tim. 2:5; Heb. 4:14-15). This union was not only for the time of Jesus ministry and sacrifice, but it is permanent and everlasting: "Jesus, because He continues forever, holds His priesthood permanently. Therefore he is able also to save forever those who draw near to God through Him, since he always lives to make intercession for them" (Heb. 7:24-25). While we cannot understand all that God has done and how the relationship between the two natures completely works, we will one day see our Savior and the wounds that He bore for us!

The fact that Jesus had both a divine nature and a human nature was an area of controversy and heresy within the early church. Nestorius, the Patriarch of Constantinople (5th century A. D.) taught that the divine nature did not associate with the human nature in Christ until birth; separating him into two persons, one of whom was God and the other man; thus a God-indwelt man rather than the "God-man."

Eutyches, a disciple of Cyril of Alexandria (5th century A.D.) in reaction to Nestorius' position taught that Jesus' human nature was absorbed into the divine nature, producing a nature that was neither human nor divine. His followers became known as monophysites ("one nature").

The Council of Calcedon (A.D. 452) addressed the heretical teaching and rendered this statement:

> "He is one Christ, existing in two natures without mixture, without division, without separation; the diversity of the natures not being destroyed by their union in the one person; but the peculiar properties of each nature being preserved and concurring to the One Person."

Not willing to completely submit to the Council's decision, some followers of Eutyches accepted the two natures of Christ but still retained their monophysite position, stating that Jesus had only one will (monothelite). That view was finally settled at the 6th Ecumenical Council of Constantinople in A.D. 680; the decision stating:

> "Jesus Christ had two distinct and inseparable wills...a human will and a divine will, working in harmony, the human in subordination to the divine: the will being regarded as an attribute of His nature rather than His person" (Whitcomb, 1982, p.54).

SACRIFICIAL DEATH OF CHRIST

One week before his arrest, trial, and crucifixion Jesus said to his disciples, including some Greeks who had come to see him, "the hour has come for the Son of Man to be glorified. Truly, truly, I say to you, unless a grain of wheat falls into the earth and dies, it remains alone; but if it dies, it bears much fruit… now My soul has become troubled; and what shall I say, 'Father, save Me from this hour'? But for this purpose I came to this hour'" (John 12:23-24, 27).

Knowing what lay before him, knowing the anguish and agony that he would soon experience, knowing the certain death that would be his, Jesus said that he would not pray for deliverance because that which he would experience in the immediate future, his suffering, death, and resurrection, were the reason he had come to earth!

IMPORTANCE OF CHRIST'S DEATH

The overall structure of this section on the death of Christ is from John C. Whitcomb, revision Christ and the Spirit theology syllabus, 1982.

OLD TESTAMENT REFERENCES AND PREDICTIONS OF THE SUFFERING AND SACRIFICE OF CHRIST

The Old Testament speaks very clearly and specifically about what the Messiah was going to do. There are at least 34 specific Old Testament references to the suffering and sacrifice of Christ.

1. Gen. 3:15 This verse has been called the Proto-Evangelium, the first proclamation of the Good News, of the Gospel. Here God is cursing the serpent because of his role in mankind's sinful act. The One whom God is going to send will "bruise the Serpent's head," but the Serpent will bruise His heel. Satan will bring about the death of the One whom God is going to send.

2. Psalm 22, a Messianic psalm written by King David about 1,000 B.C., vividly describes the suffering Christ will endure.

    a. V.1 "My God, my God, why have Your forsaken me? Far from my deliverance are the words of my groaning."

    b. VV.6-8 "But I am a worm and not a man, a reproach of men and despised by the people. All who see me sneer at me; they separate with the lip, they wag the head, saying, 'commit yourself to the Lord; let Him deliver him; let him rescue him, because He delights in him.'"

    c. VV. 14-18 "I am poured out like water; and all my bones are out of joint; My heart is like wax; it is melted within me. My strength is dried up like a potsherd, and my tongue cleaves to my jaws; and You lay me in the dust of death. For dogs have surrounded me; a band of evildoers has encompassed me; they pierced my hands and my feet. I can count all my bones. They look, they stare at me; they divide my garments among them, and for my clothing they cast lots."

3. Isa. 50:4-9; 52:13-53:12, written about 700 B.C. speaks of the Messiah/Servant's death.

a. Isa. 50:5-7 speaks in general about the humiliation that this servant will endure.

"The Lord has opened My ear; and I was not disobedient nor did I turn back. I gave My back to those who strike Me and My cheeks to those who pluck out the beard; I did not cover My face from humiliation and spitting. For the Lord God helps Me, therefore, I am not disgraced; therefore, I have set my face like flint and I know that I will not be ashamed."

b. Isa. 52:13-53:12 speaks in great detail describing how this Servant/Messiah will accomplish what He has been sent to do.

His Preeminence (52:13-15): His exaltation would be the highest, because his mistreatment would be the deepest (v.14). He will endure the furthest extent of suffering, agony, and pain so He can provide cleansing for mankind's sin (v.15).

His Person (53:1-3): While there was nothing about him to cause him to stand out above all others (vv.1-2), opposition to him would be extensive (v.3).

His Passion (53:4-6): While the world thinks it was his sin that brought this upon him, it wasn't. It was our sin that took him to the cross (v.4); our transgressions, our iniquities were the reason he went there, and the result would be our healing and the resulting peace for us. Our sin brought his piercing, crushing, punishment, wounds unto death (v.5). He did all this for those who walked away from him (v.6).

His Perseverance (53:7-9): He endured it all without complaint (v.7); suffering the unjustness of it all (v.8); remaining innocent to the end (v.9).

Results of His Sacrifice (53:10-12): God was satisfied (vv.10-11), man is declared righteous (v.11), and at the cost of His life, He won the victory (v.12).

4. Daniel 9:24-26 presents the prophecy of the 70 Weeks; during which the Messiah will be "cut off" after 62 weeks.

NEW TESTAMENT REFERENCES, REASONS FOR THE SUFFERING AND SACRIFICE OF CHRIST

1. Jesus spoke to his disciples at least three times concerning his coming death and resurrection: (1) During the year of special training of his 12 disciples; near Caesarea Philippi (Matt. 16:21), (2) a second time during that special training period, a few weeks after the first prediction (Matt. 17:22), (3) as he traveled to Jerusalem with his disciples to present himself as the King (Matt. 20:18).

2. Jesus referred to His death in his teaching on several occasions, such as (1) John 2:19 "destroy this temple, and in three days I will raise it up;" (2) John 3:14 "As Moses lifted up the serpent in the wilderness, even so must the Son of Man be lifted up;" (3) John 6:51 "the bread which I will give for the life of the world is My flesh."

3. Throughout the Epistles we see the death of Christ proclaimed.

a. Paul's letters are filled with references to Jesus' sacrificial death; seen in Romans, 1 Corinthians, Galatians, Ephesians, Colossians. It is also seen in Hebrews, 1 Peter, and 1 John.

b. The death of Christ was the foundation of the Gospel (Good News) that Paul preached (Gal. 1:6-9).

c. In his description of the Gospel, Paul said, "I delivered to you as of first importance what I also received, that Christ died for our sins according to the Scriptures..." (1 Cor. 15:3).

d. The writer of Hebrews states that the sacrifice of Jesus is better than all of the sacrifices of the Old Testament (Heb. 10:1-18).

4. The death of Christ is a guarantee of God's blessings to believers; "He who did not spare His own Son, but delivered Him over for us all, how will He not also with Him freely give us all things" (Rom. 8:32).

5. Through the death of Christ God condemned sin in the flesh and enabled us to live in obedience to and fellowship with Christ.

Rom. 8:3 "For what the Law could not do, weak as it was through the flesh, God did: sending His own Son in the likeness of sinful flesh and as an offering for sin, He condemned sin in the flesh."

Rom. 6:3-4 "Do you not know that all of us who have been baptized into Christ Jesus have been baptized into His death? Therefore we have been buried with Him through baptism into death, so that as Christ was raised from the dead through the glory of the Father, so we too might walk in newness of life."

6. The death of Christ is of great interest to the heavenly world.

   When Jesus was transfigured, Moses and Elijah met Him on the mountain, and the topic of their conversation was his coming death in Jerusalem (Luke 9:30-31).

   The angelic realm longs to look into the death of Christ and the good news it proclaims to mankind (1 Peter 1:11-12),

   When Jesus takes the scroll out of the hand of his heavenly Father, the 24 elders and 4 living creatures will fall down before him, singing "worthy are You to take the book and to break its seals; for you were slain, and purchased for God with your blood men from every tribe and tongue and people and nation" (Rev. 5:8-9).

7. As God brings His written revelation to a close with Jesus returning to defeat Satan, and end mankind's sinful rebellion against and rejection of Christ, he refers to Jesus as the Lamb at least seven times (Rev. 21:9, 14, 22, 23, 27; 22:1, 3).

NECESSITY OF CHRIST'S DEATH

SELF-IMPOSED BY JESUS

While Jesus was accused of treason and heresy by the Jewish religious leaders, condemned by the Roman governor, and put to death by the Roman soldiers, his life was not taken from him. Jesus laid down his life by his own will and choice.

John 10:17-18 "For this reason the Father loves Me, because I lay down My life so that I may take it again. No one has taken it away from Me, but I lay it down on My own initiative. I have authority to lay it down, and I have authority to take it up again. This commandment I received from My Father."

Eph. 5:2 ""Walk in love, just as Christ also loved you and gave Himself up for us, an offering and a sacrifice to God as a fragrant aroma."

Phil. 2:8 "Being found in appearance as a man, he humbled Himself by becoming obedient to the point of death, even death on a cross."

SELF-DECLARED BY JESUS

On at least three occasions Jesus declared to his disciples that He must die. Two of these occurrences were in Galilee during the special time of training for his disciples: Matt 16:21; 17:22. The third was at the end of his later Perean ministry as he traveled to Jerusalem to present Himself as the King of the Jews (Matt 20:18-19).

> Matt. 16:21 "From that time Jesus began to show His disciples that He must go to Jerusalem, and suffer many things from the elders and chief priests and scribes, and be killed, and be raised up on the third day." Jesus said that he "must" go and experience these things, The word "must" is the Greek word *dei*; the strongest Greek word to communicate necessity. Jesus said that this absolutely has to occur!

Matt. 17:22 "The Son of Man is <u>going to be</u> delivered into the hands of men; and they will kill Him, and he will be raised on the third day." The Greek word used here, *mello*, focuses not on the necessity but upon the expectation that something is about to occur.

Matt. 20:18-19 "Behold, we are going up to Jerusalem; and the Son of Man will be delivered to the chief priests and scribes, and they will condemn Him to death, and will hand Him over to the Gentiles to mock and scourge and crucify Him, and on the third day he will be raised up."

REASONS FOR THE NECESSITY OF HIS DEATH

<u>Jesus Had To Die To Fulfill His Own Eternal Purpose</u>

Rev. 13:8 "All who dwell on earth will worship him, everyone whose name has not been written from the foundation of the world in the book of life of the Lamb who has been slain."

John 12:27 Knowing that his arrest and subsequent crucifixion were only a day away, Jesus said, "now My soul has become troubled; and what shall I say, 'Father, save Me from this hour'? But for this purpose I came to this hour."

<u>Jesus Had to Die To Obey His Father's Will</u>

Six months before Jesus' arrest and crucifixion when he said to the Jews in Jerusalem that he had authority to lay his life down and authority to take it up again, he said "this commandment I received from My Father" (John 10:18).

Praying in the Garden of Gethsemane with his arrest imminent, knowing what lay before Him, Jesus said, "My Father, if it is possible, let this cup pass from Me; yet not as I will, but as You will" (Matt. 26:39). Continuing in prayer Jesus said, "My Father, if this cannot pass away unless I drink it, Your will be done" (v.44), and a short time later repeated the same thing (v.44).

Phil. 2:8 "Being found in appearance as a man, He humbled Himself by becoming obedient to the point of death, even death on a cross."

<u>Jesus Had To Die To Fulfill Prophecy</u>

When the crowd came to the Garden of Gethsemane to arrest Him, Jesus said "have you come out with swords and clubs to arrest Me as you would against a robber? Every day I used to sit in the temple teaching and you did not seize Me. But all this has taken place to fulfill the Scriptures of the prophets" (Matt. 26:55-56).

<u>Jesus Had To Die To Share His Own Eternal Life With Mankind</u>

Jesus said to Nicodemus, "truly, truly, I say to you, unless one is born again he cannot see the kingdom of God...as Moses lifted up the serpent in the wilderness, even so must the Son of Man be lifted up; so that whoever believes will in Him have eternal life" (John 3:3, 14-15).

NATURE OF CHRIST'S DEATH

God had told Adam that if he ate from the tree of the knowledge of good and evil he would surely die (Gen. 2:17); not just in the future but that very day. When Adam and Eve chose to disobey God and eat from the tree, they died that day; they died spiritually, and in time they would die physically (Gen. 5:5). The wages, payment, for sin by mankind is death (Rom. 6:23). The long-term results of Adam's sin was "death spread to all men, because all sinned" (Rom. 5:12). Physical and spiritual death were passed along to all mankind.

Without God's intervention there would have been no hope for mankind. That is exactly what he did. He gave them the Law, showing them the righteous standard that they were to meet in their life with one another and with God. Then He gave them the worship/sacrificial system by which their sins could be covered and they would be forgiven of sin. That sacrificial system required death and the offering of blood; "for the life of the flesh is in the blood, and I have given it to you on the altar to make atonement for your souls; for it is the blood by reason of the life that makes atonement" (Lev. 17:11).

As the offerings were brought, the animal was killed and the blood poured out, their sin covered over by that blood, and they were forgiven. The blood of that animal "atoned" for their sin; they were reconciled in their relationship with God. When we come to the New Testament, Jesus's death was that atonement, that reconciliation, for mankind!

CHRIST'S DEATH WAS A PHYSICAL DEATH

Jesus was beaten and whipped without mercy. Isaiah said of the Messiah, "his visage was so marred more than any man, and his form more than the sons of men" (Isa. 52:14). He was nailed to the cross so that he would physically die in excruciating pain and asphyxiation. His blood flowed, his life ebbed, and when he was ready, he gave up his spirit (John 19:30). His physical life came to an end, and his lifeless body was placed in Joseph of Arimathea's tomb.

CHRIST'S DEATH WAS A SPIRITUAL DEATH

While physical death is separation of the spirit, the soul, from the body, spiritual death is separation of the soul from God. Jesus' separation from his Father is so vividly seen in the events as he hung on the cross. During the three hours of darkness Jesus bore mankind's sins (1 Peter 2:24; Isa. 53:6; 1 John 2:2). He who was absolutely without sin was made sin for us (2 Cor. 5:21). The full extent of God's wrath was upon him (Isa. 53:10). As a man Jesus was separated from His Father, crying out "my God, my God, why have you forsaken me" (Matt. 27:46). God could not look upon the sin that Jesus bore for mankind on the cross (Hab. 1:13). In his humanity that day Jesus died spiritually in his separation from God.

MEANING OF CHRIST'S DEATH

A SUBSTITUTIONARY SACRIFICE

Throughout the Old Testament sacrificial system we see animals being sacrificed for the sins of the people (e.g Lev. 4:22-26). For almost 1,500 years thousands of animals were slain yearly and their blood poured out as an offering for sin. John the Baptist had said of Jesus, "behold, the lamb of God who takes away the sin of the world" (John 1:29). Jesus said early in his ministry that he had not come to abolish the Law or the Prophets but to fulfill them (Matt. 5:17). When he died on the cross his death did not cancel out the Old Testament sacrificial system but brought it to a conclusion. His sacrifice of Himself brought it to completion, for now no other lamb would ever have to die for the sins of mankind.

The writer of Hebrews tells us that the animal sacrifices can never make people holy, but instead they continually remind them of their sin (Heb. 10:1-3). Jesus' sacrifice is entirely different. Jesus had come to do his Father's will (Heb. 10:8), and "by this will we have been sanctified through the offering of the body of Jesus Christ once for all" (Heb. 10:10). Just as the animals were sacrificed to cover over mankind's sin, Jesus was sacrificed in our place to wash away our sin.

> Isa. 53:6 "All of us like sheep have gone astray, each of us has turned to his own way; but the Lord has caused the iniquity of us all to fall on him."

> 2 Cor. 5:21 "He made Him who knew no sin to be sin on our behalf, so that we might become the righteousness of God in Him."

> 1 Peter 3:18 "For Christ also died for sins once for all, the just for the unjust, so that he might bring us to God, having been put to death in the flesh but made alive in the spirit."

A RECONCILIATION

Reconciliation implies the removal of opposition, strife, enmity between persons; that which has separated them is removed and the relationship is restored. The need for this reconciliation with God is seen in Isaiah's words, "your iniquities have made a separation between you and your God, and your sins have hidden His face from you so that he does not hear" (Isa. 59:2). Christ's death has provided the way by which we can be reconciled to God.

> Rom. 5:10-11 "For if while we were enemies we were reconciled to God through the death

of His Son, much more, having been reconciled, we shall be saved by his life. And not only this, but we also exult in God through our Lord Jesus Christ, through whom we have now received the reconciliation."

2 Cor. 5:18-19 "God reconciled us to Himself through Christ…reconciling the world to Himself, not counting their trespasses against them."

Eph. 2:16 "That He might reconcile them both (Jew and Gentile) in one body to God through the cross, by it having put to death the enmity."

Col. 1:19-20 "It was the Father's good pleasure for all the fullness to dwell in Him, and through Him to reconcile all things to Himself, having made peace through the blood of His cross."

A PROPITIATION

Propitiation (Grk "*hilasterion*") is the place where God is appeased, satisfied. In the Old Testament that place was the Mercy Seat (cover of the Ark of the Covenant) in the Holy of Holies. There, on the Day of Atonement, the blood of the sacrificial animal was sprinkled for the sins of the people. That covering lid was the place where God was satisfied with the sacrificial offering.

In the New Testament that place of propitiation is no longer the Mercy Seat, but it is the Lord Jesus Christ. It is in Jesus' sacrifice on the cross that God the Father is appeased, satisfied, the sacrifice sufficient for all sin!

Rom. 3:24b-25 "the redemption which is in Christ Jesus; whom God displayed publicly as a propitiation in His blood through faith."

Heb. 2:17 "therefore, He had to be made like His brethren in all things, so that he might become a merciful and faithful high priest in things pertaining to God, to make propitiation for the sins of the people."

1 John 2:2 "He himself is the propitiation for our sins; and not for ours only, but also for those of the whole world."

1 John 4:10 "In this is love, not that we loved God, but that he loved us and sent His son to be the propitiation for our sins."

A REDEMPTION

There is a cost for mankind's sin as Paul has so vividly stated: "for the wages of sin is death" (Rom. 6:23a). Because of Adam's and our willful sin we stand guilty before God, and the consequences of that sin must be faced; must be paid! Either man pays it himself when he stands in judgment before God, or it is paid through a substitute; see Substitutionary Sacrifice above. That which Jesus Christ did on the cross was to pay the price, the cost, of our sin.

Matt. 20:28 "The Son of Man did not come to be served, but to serve, and to give His life a ransom for many."

Acts 20:28 "the church of God which he purchased with His own blood."

Rom. 3:24 "Being justified as a gift by His grace through the redemption which is in Christ Jesus."

1 Peter 1:18-19 "Knowing that you were not redeemed with perishable things like silver or gold from your futile way of life inherited from your forefathers, but with precious blood, as of a lamb unblemished and spotless, the blood of Christ."

RESULTS OF CHRIST'S SACRIFICE

RESULTS IN RELATION TO BELIEVERS

1. Redeemed us from the curse of law (Gal. 3:13)

   "Christ redeemed us from the curse of the Law, having become a curse for us- for it is written, 'cursed is everyone who hangs on a tree.'"

2. Loosed us from our sins (Rev. 1:5)

   "And from Jesus Christ, the faithful witness, the firstborn of the dead, and the ruler of the kings of the earth. To Him who loves us and released us from our sins by His blood."

3. Purchased us for God (Rev. 5:9)

   "Worthy are You to take the book and to break its seals; for you were slain, and purchased for God with Your blood men from every tribe and tongue and people and nation."

4. Brought us near to God (Eph. 2:13)

   "But now in Christ Jesus you who formerly were far off have been brought near by the blood of Christ."

5. Secured eternal life for us (John 3:14-15)

   "As Moses lifted up the serpent in the wilderness, even so must the Son of Man be lifted up; so that whoever believes will in Him have eternal life."

6. Justified us by His blood (Rom. 5:9)

   "Much more then, having now been justified by His blood, we shall be saved from the wrath of God through Him."

7. Sanctified us by His blood (Heb. 10:10)

   "By this will we have been sanctified through the offering of the body of Jesus Christ once for all."

8. Made us perfect in God's sight (Heb. 10:14)

   "For by one offering He has perfected for all time those who are sanctified."

9. Opened a way for us into the presence of God (Heb. 10:19-20)

   "Therefore, brethren, since we have confidence to enter the holy place by the blood of Jesus, by a new and living way which he inaugurated for us through the veil, that is, His flesh."

10. Made it impossible to condemn us (Rom. 8:33–34)

"Who will bring a charge against God's elect? God is the one who justifies; who is the one condemns? Christ Jesus is He who died, yes, rather who was raised, who is at the right hand of God, who also intercedes for us."

11. Cleanses us constantly from all sin (1 John 1:7)

"But if we walk in the Light as He Himself is in the Light, we have fellowship with one another, and the blood of Jesus His Son cleanses us from all sin."

12. Made us fit to dwell with God in heaven (Rev. 7:14)

"These are the ones who come out of the great tribulation, and they have washed their robes and made them white in the blood of the Lamb."

RESULTS IN RELATION TO THE WHOLE HUMAN RACE

He has reconciled the world to God. Because of Jesus' sacrifice the door is open for all to come to God.

2 Cor. 5:19 "God was in Christ reconciling the world to Himself."

1 John 2:2 "He Himself is the propitiation for our sins; and not for ours only, but also for those of the whole world."

RESULTS IN RELATION TO SATAN AND HIS HOSTS

Satan has been cast out and rendered powerless in believers' lives.

> John 12:31 "Now judgment is upon this world; now the ruler of this world will be cast out."

> Heb. 2:14-15 "...that through death He might render powerless him who had the power of death, that is, the devil, and might free those who through fear of death were subject to slavery all their lives."

RESULTS IN RELATION TO THE UNIVERSE

Even the things in heaven had to be cleansed by the blood of Christ (Heb. 9:22-23).

Col. 1:20 "Through Him to reconcile all things to Himself, having made peace through the blood of His cross; through Him, I say, whether things on earth or things in heaven."

RESULTS IN RELATION TO CHRIST (AS MEDIATOR)

1. Fulfilled his part in the Covenant with His Father (Heb. 13:20- His blood is the basis of that covenant).
2. Laid the foundation of His priestly work (Heb. 9:11-12- by His own blood he entered in once into the Holy Place).
3. Secured His exaltation above all (Phil. 2:8-9 God has highly exalted Him and given Him a name above all names).
4. Crowned Him with glory and honor (Heb. 2:9- crowned because of His death so that by God's grace He might taste death for everyone).

RESULTS IN RELATION TO GOD

1. Revealed God's love for sinners (Rom. 5:8).

   "God demonstrates His own love toward us, in that while we were yet sinners, Christ died for us."

2. Revealed God's righteousness in forgiving sin (Rom. 3:25).

   "This was to demonstrate His righteousness, because in the forbearance of God He passed over the sins previously committed."

3. Revealed God's wrath against sin (Matt. 27:46).

   "About the ninth hour Jesus cried out with a loud voice, saying, *'eli eli, lama sabachthani?*, that is My God, My God, why have You forsaken Me?"

4. Revealed God's wisdom in providing a way to save sinners (Rom. 3:26).

   "For the demonstration, I say, of his righteousness at the present time, so that He would be just and the justifier of the one who has faith in Jesus."

The sacrificial death of Christ can be summed up in these three simple verses: "For God so loved the world, that he gave His only begotten Son, that whoever believes in Him shall not perish, but have eternal life. For God did not send the Son into the world to judge the world, but that the world might be saved through Him (John 3:16-17)…"Christ died for sins once for all, the just for the unjust, so that he might bring us to God, having been put to death in the flesh, but made alive in the spirit" (1 Peter 3:18).

RESURRECTION AND ASCENSION OF CHRIST

RESURRECTION OF CHRIST

Each of the times that Jesus told his disciples that he was going to be arrested, beaten, and killed he also said that he was going to be raised from the dead (Matt. 16:21; 17:22-23; Luke 18:31-33). As certain as his death, so also was the certainty of his resurrection. As necessary as the death of Jesus, so also was the necessity of his resurrection.

The apostle Paul stated, "if Christ has not been raised, your faith is worthless; you are still in your sins. Then those who have fallen asleep in Christ have perished" (1 Cor. 15:17-18). Paul earlier in that letter in his description of the Gospel said, "for I delivered to you as of first importance what I also received, that Christ died for our sins according to the Scriptures, and that he was buried, and that He was raised on the third day according to the Scriptures" (1 Cor. 15:3-4). The resurrection of Jesus Christ was not simply something that God did as an afterthought, but it is an essential vital part of the cross-work of Christ. Belief in Jesus' resurrection is an essential part of our salvation: "if you confess with your mouth Jesus as Lord, and believe in your heart that God raised him from the dead, you will be saved; for with the heart a person believes, resulting in righteousness, and with the mouth he confesses, resulting in salvation" (Rom. 10:9-10).

OLD TESTAMENT PROPHECIES OF CHRIST'S RESURRECTION

The resurrection of Christ is predicted in these two messianic psalms; each of which is referred to in the book of Acts.

> Psalm 16:10 "For You will not abandon my soul to Sheol; nor will You allow Your Holy One to undergo decay." Quoted in Peter's sermon on the Day of Pentecost (Acts 2:24-28) and Paul's sermon in Antioch of Pisidia (Acts 13:16-31)

> Psalm 2:7 "I will surely tell of the decree of the Lord: He said to Me, 'You are My Son, today I have begotten You.'" Quoted in Paul's sermon in Antioch of Pisidia (Acts 13:33).

NEW TESTAMENT TESTIMONY OF CHRIST'S RESURRECTION

Jesus' Testimony of His Resurrection

John 2:19 Answering those who asked him about his authority to cleanse the temple, Jesus said, "destroy this temple, and in three days I will raise it up."

John 10:17-18 "For this reason the Father loves Me, because I lay down My life so that I may take it again. No one has taken it away from me, but I lay it down on My own initiative. I have authority to lay it down, and I have authority to take it up again This commandment I received from my Father."

Jesus directly proclaimed to his disciples about his coming arrest, abuse, death and resurrection: Matt. 16:21; 17:22-23; Luke 18:33.

Matt. 17:9 At his transfiguration Moses and Elijah came down to talk with Jesus about his coming departure (crucifixion, death, and resurrection) in Jerusalem. As Jesus and his three disciples descended the mountain Jesus said, "tell the vision to no one until the Son of Man has risen from the dead" (Matt. 17:9).

Matt. 25:31ff In His teaching on the Mt. of Olives to four of his disciples Jesus said, "when the Son of Man comes in His glory, and all the angels with Him, then He will sit on His glorious throne..." This will occur when Jesus returns to set up his Kingdom on the earth.

Matt. 26:64 In his trial before Caiaphas Jesus said, "hereafter you will see the Son of Man sitting at the right hand of power, and coming on the clouds of heaven."

Testimony of New Testament Writers

Every New Testament writer spoke of Jesus' resurrection: Matthew (ch.28), Mark (16:1-8), Luke (Luke 24, Acts 1), John (John 20-21, Revelation), Paul (all his epistles), Peter (1 Peter 1:3), James (5:7), Jude (v.14).

THEOLOGICAL SIGNIFICANCE OF CHRIST'S RESURRECTION

Broke Satan's Power Over Death

Heb. 2:14 "Since the children share in flesh and blood, He Himself (Jesus) likewise also partook of the same, that through death he might render powerless him who had the power of death, that is, the devil". Satan's death grip upon man was now over; Christ's sacrifice brought redemption for mankind, and his resurrection guaranteed that "in Christ all will be made alive" (1 Cor. 15:22).

Fulfills Promise to Old Testament Fathers

God had made promises to Abraham (Gen. 12:3; 22:18), Isaac (Gen. 26:4) which could not be fulfilled if Jesus was not resurrected.

Validates the Claims Jesus Made

Some of his claims are noted: John 2:19-21; 5:17-18; 10:17-18.

Paul writes of Jesus, "His Son, who was born of a descendant of David according to the flesh, who was declared the Son of God with power by the resurrection from the dead, according to the Spirit of holiness, Jesus Christ our Lord" (Rom. 1:3-4).

Validates Christ's Atoning Work

Paul stated, "Christ was delivered over because of our transgressions" (Rom. 4:25a), and because of that we are justified by his blood (Rom. 5:9), also "He was raised because of our justification" (Rom. 4:25b). The work he had come to do, man's justification, had been accomplished, and now Christ was raised from the dead.

Guarantees the Believer's Future Resurrection

1 Cor. 15:20-23 "But now Christ has been raised from the dead, the first fruits of those who are asleep. For since by a man came death, by a man also came the resurrection of the dead. For as in Adam all die, so also in Christ all will be made alive. But each in his own order: Christ the first fruits, after that those who are Christ's at his coming."

Guarantees the Final Judgment of Mankind

Acts 17:31 Speaking to the people in Athens Paul said, "God has fixed a day in which He will judge the world in righteousness through a Man whom he has appointed, having furnished proof to all men by raising Him from the dead."

<u>Pattern for Believer's Future Bodies</u>

Phil. 3:20-21 "For our citizenship is in heaven, from which also we eagerly wait for a Savior, the Lord Jesus Christ; who will transform the body of our humble state into conformity with the body of His glory, by the exertion of the power that he has even to subject all things to Himself."

WITNESSES TO CHRIST'S RESURRECTION

1. Witness of the angels at the empty tomb (Luke 24:4-8).
2. Witness of the women who had come to take care of Jesus' body: Mary Magdalene, Mary the mother of James, Salome, Johanna, and others (Mark 16:1).
3. Witness of Peter and John who run to the tomb, find it empty, and then return to their homes (John 20:3-10).
4. Witness of Mary Magdalene who remained and saw Jesus; though telling the others she was not believed (John 20:11-18; Mark 16:10-11).
5. Witness of the other women who met the Lord and worshipped Him and took his message back to the others (Matt 28:9-10).
6. Witness of the guards to the chief priests; who bribed them (Matt. 28:11-15).
7. Witness of the two disciples on the Emmaus road (Luke 24:13-35).
8. Witness of the ten disciples in a home in Jerusalem (John 20:19-25).
9. Witness of the eleven assembled disciples, including Thomas (John 20:26-31).

10. Witness of the eleven disciples who were fishing (John 21:1-25).
11. Witness of the eleven disciples who had gathered at a mountain in Galilee (Matt. 28:16-20).
12. Witness of many over the 40 days after his resurrection (Acts 1:3-8).

ASCENSION OF CHRIST

Forty days after His resurrection Jesus departed physically and visibly from the earth and immediately entered Heaven (Mark 16:19-20; Luke 24:50-53; Acts 1:6-12).

PROPHESIED IN THE OLD TESTAMENT

Psalm 68:18 "You have ascended on high, You have led captive Your captives; You have received gifts among men..." Quoted in Eph. 4:8.

Psalm 110:1 "The Lord says to my Lord: 'sit at My right hand until I make your enemies a footstool for your feet.'" Quoted in Peter's sermon in Acts 2:34-35.

Isa. 52:13 "Behold, My servant will prosper, He will be high and lifted up and greatly exalted."

SPOKEN OF BY JESUS

John 7:33 "For a little while longer I am with you, then I go to Him who sent Me. You will seek Me, and will not find Me; and where I am, you cannot come."

John 8:21 "Then He said again to them, 'I go away, and you will seek Me, and will die in your sin; where I am going, you cannot come.'"

John 14:28-29 "I go to the Father...I have told you before it happens, so that when it happens, you may believe."

John 16:5 "But now I am going to Him who sent Me."

DESCRIBED AS A PHYSICAL HISTORICAL EVENT SEEN BY OTHERS

Forty days after His resurrection the disciples were gathered with Jesus on the Mount of Olives. While he was talking with them He began to rise from the earth into the sky. Jesus did not simply disappear from their sight; they watched as He arose from the earth into the clouds. As they continued looking on a cloud quickly prevented them from seeing him any further. Yet, while they continued looking up two angels appeared and said, "Men of Galilee, why do you stand looking into the sky? This Jesus, who has been taken up from you into heaven, will come in just the same way as you have watched Him go into heaven" (Acts 1:10-11). Here was both a sad separation and a hope-filled future; He was gone to heaven now, but He will return as He promised!

Acts 1:9 "After He had said these things, He was lifted up while they were looking on, and a cloud received Him out of their sight."

Mark 16:19 "So then, when the Lord Jesus had spoken to them, He was received up into heaven and sat down at the right hand of God."

IMPORTANCE OF JESUS' ASCENSION

Jesus' ascension marked the end of His first advent and completion of that which he had been sent to do. "When he had made purification of sins, He sat down at the right hand of the Majesty on high" (Heb. 1:3a).

Jesus' ascension exalted him as head over all things. "The working of the strength of God's might which He brought about in Christ, when he raised Him from the dead and seated Him at His right hand in the heavenly places, far above all rule and authority and power and dominion, and every name that is named, not only in this age but also in the one to come. And he put all things in subjection under His feet, and gave Him as head over all things to the church..." (Eph. 1:20-22).

Jesus' ascension made possible his present priestly work in Heaven. He is our high priest in the presence of God (Heb. 7:26; 8:1-4). He is our advocate at the right hand of God, and because of that we can come into the very presence of God through him; receiving mercy and grace in our time of need (Heb. 4:14-16).

Jesus' ascension guarantees His triumph over all His enemies. "The Lord said to My Lord 'sit at My right hand, until I make Your enemies a footstool for Your feet'" (Acts 2:34-35). All of mankind's rebellion will be stopped, judged, and Jesus will rule over all of creation!

Jesus' ascension allowed the Holy Spirit to do the work that He was to do during this church age. In the Upper Room the night of his arrest Jesus said that he had to go; he could not remain there but was going to prepare a place for them. Yet, He would not leave them alone but God would send another comforter to teach them and remind them of all that Jesus said (John 14:25). Jesus said that if He did not go away from them, the Holy Spirit would not come to them; but if He went, then he would send the Holy Spirit to them (John 16:7). Jesus' ascension made the Holy Spirit's coming not only a hope but a reality!

RETURN AND REIGN OF CHRIST

Depending on the system of biblical chronology one uses, the dates of Jesus' death, burial, and resurrection may be placed between A.D. 30-33. Sixty plus years later the apostle John was in exile on the Isle of Patmos in the southeast Aegean Sea. There he received his vision regarding the End-Time events for mankind, God's judgment, and Christ's rule upon this earth. In that vision John also saw the glorified Lord! At the end of all that John was shown, three times these words were said by and about Jesus, "Behold, I am coming soon" (Rev.22:7, 12, 20).

Almost 2,000 years have passed since those events, and Jesus has not returned yet. His return is much nearer now than it was at John's time on Patmos, nearer than Martin Luther's time, nearer than it was even five years ago. While he ascended to heaven after his resurrection, that is not the final role of Jesus Christ for mankind and this world. Jesus is going to return, resurrect mankind from their graves, reward the righteous, rule over all creation for 1,000 years, judge the wicked-Satan- and his evil angels, and establish the eternal rule of righteousness under his Father.

As we consider Jesus' return and reign there are several individual components that sequentially occur. These will be considered in the basic order in which they occur.

FAULTY THEORIES OF CHRIST'S SECOND COMING

SPIRITUAL THEORY

This view states Jesus came in the Holy Spirit at Pentecost. This view confuses the spiritual presence of Christ with the physical, bodily, visible presence of Christ in the same body in which he ascended. It was the Holy Spirit who came at Pentecost (Acts 2). Refutation: Peter was still looking forward to Christ's return in Acts 3:19-20.

JUDGMENT THEORY

This view states that he came in judgment of Jerusalem in A.D. 70. Refutation: the Book of Revelation was written more than 25 years after Jerusalem's destruction, and there John the author states that Jesus' coming is still future (Rev. 22:7, 12).

CONVERSION THEORY

This view states he comes into the believer's heart. This is true to the extent he comes spiritually into a person's heart at conversion, but it confuses his spiritual presence with his physical coming. Refutation: Phil. 3:20-21 states we look forward to Christ's coming when he will change/conform our bodies to be like his glorified body. That has not happened yet!

DEATH THEORY

This view states that Jesus comes to get us when we die. When Stephen was going to be stoned to death he looked into heaven and saw Jesus standing at the right hand of God (Acts 7:55-56). Within a few moments he was in Jesus' presence! This view confuses this reception of believers at death with Jesus' bodily return. Refutation: 1 Thess. 4:13-17; both the dead and the living will be taken up to meet the Lord in the air.

POST-MILLENNIAL THEORY

This view states that Jesus is going to come after the Millennium. It states the gospel will slowly bring the world to Christ; making it increasingly better, thus enabling Jesus to return to rule, reward the righteous, and judge sinners. Refutation: Rev. 19:11-20:6 which shows Jesus coming at Armageddon, judging the Beast and False Prophet, binding Satan, and then establishing his reign for 1,000 years.

A-MILLENNIAL THEORY

This view states there is no millennium. It states good and evil will develop side-by-side. At the end Jesus will literally and visibly return to end man's rule and usher in eternity. Refutation: Rev. 20:4-6 those who were martyred for Christ during the Tribulation, and those raptured before will reign with Jesus Christ for 1,000 years!

BIBLICAL DOCTRINE OF CHRIST'S SECOND COMING

SECOND COMING IN THE OLD TESTAMENT

The Old Testament speaks much of the Messiah's coming (e.g. Gen. 3:15; 49:10; 2 Sam. 7:12-13; Micah 5:2; Isa. 7:14), over 300 references refer to his second coming. These prophecies present two different predictions about the Messiah. One, he will be a great, powerful, ruling king (Isa. 9:6-7; 11:1-5; Jer. 23:5-8; Daniel 7:13-14; Malachi 3:1-2). The other, he will be lowly, suffering, rejected (Psalm 22:1, 14-18; Isa. 53:2-9; Daniel 9:26; Zech. 13:7).

The Old Testament Jew wrestled extensively with these two distinctly different views, and the prophets searched their own writings seeking to understand what was going to occur. Jesus himself clarified the views by saying he is fulfilling both: suffering and rejected in his first coming (Luke 24:26) and then power and glory when he returns (Matt. 24:30).

All of the prophecies not fulfilled at His first coming will be fulfilled when he returns. For every Old Testament prophecy of his first coming there are eight for his second coming.

SECOND COMING IN THE NEW TESTAMENT

While the term Second Coming does not occur in the New Testament, the idea itself is clearly stated. Jesus said, "I will come again" (John 14:3), and the writer of Hebrews stated, "Christ shall appear a second time" (Heb. 9:28). At least eight different terms are used in the New Testament to speak of Jesus' second coming.

<u>Distinctives of Jesus' Second Coming</u>

1. Christ will come in person.

    Acts 1:11 "Men of Galilee, why do you stand looking into the sky? This Jesus, who has been taken up from you into heaven, will come in just the same way as you have watched Him go into heaven."

    1 Thess. 4:16 "For the Lord Himself will descend from heaven with a shout, with the voice of the archangel and with the trumpet of God, and the dead in Christ will rise first."

2. Christ will come literally and visibly.

> Rev. 1:7 "Behold, he is coming with the clouds, and every eye will see Him, even those who pierced Him..."

> 1 John 3:2 "We know that when he appears, we will be like Him, because we will see Him just as He is."

> Zech. 14:3-4 "Then the Lord will go forth and fight against those nations, as when He fights on a day of battle. In that day His feet will stand on the Mount of Olives..."

3. Christ will come in glory.

> John 1:14 "The Word became flesh and dwelt among us, and we saw His glory, glory as of the only begotten from the Father, full of grace and truth."

> John 17:5 "Now Father, glorify Me together with yourself, with the glory which I had with You before the world was."

> Matt. 16:27 "For the Son of Man is going to come in the glory of His Father with His angels, and will then repay every man according to his deeds."

> Matt. 24:30 "And then the sign of the Son of Man will appear in the sky, and then all the tribes of the earth will mourn, and they will see the Son of Man coming on the clouds of the sky with power and great glory."

> Matt. 25:31 "When the Son of Man comes in His glory and all the angels with Him, then he will sit on His glorious throne."

4. Christ will come in power.

Matt. 24:30 "And then the sign of the Son of Man will appear in the sky, and then all the tribes of the earth will mourn, and they will see the Son of Man coming on the clouds of the sky with power and great glory."

Matt. 26:64 In his trial before the high priest Jesus said, "I tell you hereafter you will see the Son of Man sitting at the right hand of power and coming on the clouds of heaven."

When Christ returns He will defeat all opposing him; all angelic realms and all mankind. The Beast and False Prophet will be cast alive into the Lake of Fire (Rev. 19:20); Satan will be bound with a chain and cast into the abyss for 1,000 years (Rev. 20:1-3); rebellious mankind will be defeated (Rev. 19:11-18). Mankind's final rebellion with Satan leading them will be defeated; Satan will be cast into the Lake of Fire, and mankind judged and cast into the Lake of Fire.

5. Christ will come attended by angels.

Matt. 25:31 "When the Son of Man comes in His glory, and all the angels with Him, then he will sit on His glorious throne."

Rev. 5:11 "Then I looked, and I heard the voice of many angels around the throne and the living creatures and the elders; and the number of them was myriads of myriads, and thousands of thousands."

When Jesus explained to his disciples the parable of the tares in the field, he said, "so just as the tares are gathered up and burned with fire, so shall it be at the end of the age. The Son of Man will send forth His angels, and they will gather out of his kingdom all stumbling blocks, and those who commit lawlessness, and will throw them into the furnace of fire; in that place there will be weeping and gnashing of teeth. Then the righteous will shine forth as the sun in the kingdom of their Father" (Matt. 13:40-43).

When the Lord returns to rule and reign, millions of angels will come with him. They will come to gather out of mankind all wicked people (Matt. 13:41-43), to minister to those who are saved (Matt. 18:10; Heb. 1:14), and to serve King Jesus (Matt. 25:31). When Jesus returns all the nations will be gathered before him, and "He will separate them from one another, as the shepherd separates the sheep from the goats...to those on His right he will say 'come, you who are blessed of My Father, inherit the kingdom prepared for you from the foundation of the world'... to those on His left, 'depart from me, accursed ones, into the eternal fire which has been prepared for the devil and his angels'...these will go away into eternal punishment, but the righteous into eternal life" (Matt. 25:32, 34, 41, 46). The myriad of angels will escort the believers into Christ's kingdom, and they will take the others to their eternal punishment.

6. Christ will come quickly (Rev. 22:7, 12, 20).

Rev. 22:7, 12, 20 "And behold, I am coming quickly... behold, I am coming quickly, and My reward is with Me, to render to every man according to what he has done... Yes, I am coming quickly!"

7. Christ will come unexpectedly.

> Luke 21:34-35 "Be on guard, so that your hearts will not be weighed down with dissipation and drunkenness and the worries of life, and that day will not come on you suddenly like a trap; for it will come upon all those who dwell on the face of all the earth."

> When the Lord returns to end tribulation, stop Satan's works and control of people, all mankind will be simply trying to live. Those who are Christ's will be struggling to survive, and those who are not will be going about their daily lives in exclusion of Jesus. The believers will be hoping, but the rest of the world will have no thought of Jesus' return.

8. Christ will come in two main phases:

    a. He will come <u>for</u> His church (1 Thess. 4:15-18)
    b. He will come <u>with</u> His Church (1 Thess. 3:13; 2 Thess. 1:7-10)

Time of Christ's Second Coming (Day of the Lord)

1. No time is given in Scripture.

> In the Olivet Discourse Jesus said, "of that day or hour no one knows, not even the angels in heaven, nor the Son, <u>but the Father alone</u>" (Mark 13:32; see also Matt. 24:36). Just before his ascension the disciples asked Jesus, "Lord, is it at this time You are restoring the kingdom to Israel" (Acts 1:6). Jesus answered, "it is not for you to know times or epochs which <u>the Father has fixed by His</u>

own authority" (Acts 1:7). No time is given in Scripture; no date can be set by anyone!

2. The time is always imminent.

    No clearly predicted event must occur before the Lord comes back to receive His church to Himself. We eagerly await His return and are to be alert, ever watchful and waiting (1 Thess. 5:6; Titus 2:13). "Christ also, having been offered once to bear the sins of many, will appear a second time for salvation without reference to sin, to those who eagerly await Him" (Heb. 9:28).

3. Why has God waited so long?

    "The Lord is not slow about his promise, as some count slowness, but is patient toward you, not wishing for any to perish but for all to come to repentance" (2 Peter 3:9).

CHRIST COMING FOR HIS CHURCH: THE RAPTURE

Descriptive Terms for The Rapture

It is referred to as the receiving (John 14:3), the adoption and redemption (Rom. 8:23), the change (1 Cor. 15:51), the upward call (Phil. 3:14), the catching up (1 Thess. 4:17), the gathering (2 Thess. 2:1), the keeping (Rev. 3:10).

Details of the Rapture (1 Thess. 4:13-18)

1. The rapture is the first event related to the Second Coming. No other end-times event precedes it, and no signs or warnings are given prior to it.

2. Jesus' descent from heaven (v.16)

He will personally come from heaven to the earth's atmosphere (v.17). With him when he comes are those church saints who had already died and gone to be with him (v.14; 2 Cor. 5:6-8).

3. Jesus comes with a "shout" (v.16)

This is literally a shout of command. Standing at Lazarus' tomb Jesus loudly commanded "Lazarus, come forth" (John 11:43), and Lazarus immediately rose from the dead. To those criticizing him for healing a man on the Sabbath Jesus said, "truly, truly, I say to you, an hour is coming and now is, when the dead will hear the voice of the Son of God, and those who hear will live…do not marvel at this; for an hour is coming, in which all who are in the tombs will hear his voice, and will come forth; those who did good deeds to a resurrection of life, those who committed the evil deeds to a resurrection of Judgment" (John 5:25, 28-29).

When Jesus returns he will command the bodies of believers in the graves to arise, and they will be the first to meet the Lord in the air and after them the living believers (1 Thess. 4:15-16). Their bodies are changed from decay to glorious bodies; "we will not all sleep, but we will all be changed…the dead will be raised imperishable, and we will be changed" (1 Cor. 15:51-52). No true believer will be left behind!

4. Jesus comes with the voice of the archangel (v.16)

Michael, the highest of God's righteous created beings will be there; announcing Christ's presence. He protected

Israel in Daniel's day (Daniel 10:13, 21), will protect Israel during the Tribulation (Daniel 12:1), and has defeated Satan and his demonic host, casting them to the earth (Rev. 12:7-9).

5. Jesus comes with the trumpet of God (v.16)

    The trumpet was used in the Old Testament to assemble the nation of Israel. Jesus is calling all God's people to himself; those he is calling from the grave and from the living of the earth, joining the saints He has brought with him.

Time of the Rapture

There are at least three wrong theories of the rapture's timing:

- Post-Tribulation rapture: teaches Christ comes for his church after the judgments in Rev. 4-19.
- Mid-Tribulation rapture: states the trumpet in 1 Thess. 4:16 is the same as the 7th trumpet sounded during the Tribulation; thus making this somewhere mid-way in the Tribulation period events.
- Partial rapture: states that only believers who are watching and waiting for Christ's return will be raptured when he comes in the air. Those believers who are carnal will be left to go through the Tribulation; being sanctified through its events and horrors. They will then be raptured when they are ready or just before Christ returns to put down all rebellion and set up his kingdom.

The correct view of the rapture's timing is the Pre-tribulation rapture. This view states that the church in its entirety is raptured before the revelation of the Antichrist and the beginning of the events of this seven year Tribulation period. In Rev. 3:10 Jesus said to the church of Philadelphia, "I will keep you from the hour of testing, that hour which is about to come upon the whole world, to test those who dwell on the earth." Also, there is no mention of the church in Rev. 4:1-19:7. The Tribulation period is to prepare the world for Christ's Second coming, with the gospel going across the entire world, including Israel who during this time will recognize they missed their Messiah and will come to Him in faith.

A significant variation of this view is the Pre-Wrath view; stating that the first four seals opened are really Satan's activity, and that God's wrath does not begin until the fifth seal is opened. This view has the church experiencing great suffering through the events of these first four seals.

Two days before his arrest Jesus' disciples asked him what would be the sign of His coming (Matt.24:3). Jesus said great suffering was coming: great deception, wars and rumors of wars, famines and earthquakes, and these are merely the beginning of birth pains" (Matt. 24:5-8). Since mankind's sin in the Garden of Eden Satan has been the prince of demons (Luke 11:15), the prince of the power of the air (Eph. 2:2), the ruler of this world (John 12:31; 14:30). It is now time for his influence on God's creation, his rule to come to an end. When Jesus begins to open the seals on the scroll, it is now time for God's judgment to come to this sinful world and the one, Satan, who continually corrupts it. Jesus does not need to use Satan or the antichrist to bring any more chaos on the world or even to be His arm of judgment. As Jesus begins opening the seals it is His judgment that begins to come. The pre-wrath view does not recognize this and consequently should be rejected!

CHURCH GOING TO THE FATHER'S HOUSE

In the Upper Room the night of His arrest Jesus said to his disciples, "do not let your heart be troubled; believe in God, believe also in me. In My Father's house are many dwelling places; if it were not so, I would have told you; for I go to prepare a place for you. If I go and prepare a place for you I will come again and receive you to myself that where I am, there you may be also" (John 14:1-3). Heaven is God's dwelling place (2 Chron. 6:30). This heavenly city will be the church's dwelling during the Millennial kingdom. While we will reign with Christ over the earth during the Millennium (Rev. 5:10), our home will be in heaven.

At the end of the Millennium that holy city, New Jerusalem will come down out of heaven to earth (Rev. 21:1-3, 10) where it will remain for all eternity. "Behold, the tabernacle of God is among men, and he will dwell among them, and they shall be His people, and God Himself will be among them" (v.3).

JUDGMENT SEAT OF CHRIST AND MARRIAGE SUPPER OF THE LAMB

While the events of the seven year Tribulation period are occurring on earth, the church is being sanctified and perfected by Jesus. Eph. 5:25-27 "Husbands, love your wives, just as Christ also loved the church and gave Himself up for her, so that he might sanctify her, having cleansed her by the washing of water with the word, that he might present to himself the church in all her glory, having no spot or wrinkle or any such thing; but that she would be holy and blameless."

In the Father's House the church appears before the Judgement Seat of Christ, where each member of the church will give an account of himself to God (Rom. 14:10-13). "For we must all appear before the judgment seat of Christ so that each one may be recompensed for his deeds in the body according to what he has done, whether good or bad" (2 Cor. 5:10).

While the church, the body of Christ has been sanctified, she is still being daily sanctified as she walks in this world. When the day comes that Jesus takes the church, his bride, to his Father's house, he begins the final part of her sanctification; removing every spot marring her holiness, rewarding her for that which she has done, and clothing her with the righteous acts of the saints (Rev. 19:7-8). Then just before Jesus returns to defeat and destroy all wickedness the marriage supper of the Lamb occurs (Rev. 19:6-9).

TRIBULATION EVENTS

With the church gone, the next steps in God's program for the end-times begin to unfold; the prophecies of Daniel will now be fulfilled (Daniel 7:8, 19-26; 9:24-27; 11:36-45). The Lawless one, the Antichrist, will now be revealed (2 Thess. 2:1-12). Quickly seizing political power, he will make a treaty with the Jews (Daniel 9:27), which marks the beginning of Daniel's 70th week; only to break it 3 ½ years later. Stopping temple worship, he will set himself up in the temple to be worshipped (2 Thess. 2:4). Here the Jews realize their mistake, turn from him, and turn to Christ. For the next 3 ½ years the antichrist persecutes the Jews and believers; seeking to destroy all.

As the Antichrist is doing this, God is progressively pouring out His judgement upon this world system through three series of judgments: seven seals, seven trumpets, and seven bowls of God's wrath. When the seventh bowl of wrath is poured out, world power and false world religion are destroyed (Rev. 17-18), with heaven rejoicing in the events (Rev. 19:1-6).

CHRIST'S PHYSICAL RETURN (REV. 19:11-21)

Jesus will return with his armies (his saints) to end all rebellion and oppression, all sin (Zech. 14:5). On his robe is written "King of kings, and Lord of lords" (Rev. 19:16). The armies of the world will have gathered with the Antichrist to battle Christ (Rev. 19:19). Their great pride and plans are absolutely futile in the coming of Jesus Christ. The Antichrist and the false prophet are taken and cast alive into the lake of fire (Rev. 19:20). Then, all of the armies that had gathered against Christ will be killed by the sword that comes from His mouth (Rev. 19:21). And God said!!!

REIGN OF CHRIST

"The Lord will be king over all the earth; in that day the Lord will be the only one, and His name the only one" (Zech. 14:9).

CHRIST'S THRONE

When God made a covenant with David He said, "I will make you a great name; like the names of the great men who are on earth... I will appoint a place for my people Israel and will plant them... the Lord will make a house for you. When your days are complete and you lie down with your fathers, I will raise up your descendant after you, who will come forth from you, and I will establish his kingdom. He shall build a house for my name, and I will establish the throne of his kingdom forever" (2 Sam. 9-13).

Seven hundred years before the birth of the promised Messiah, Isaiah said, "for a child will be born to us, a son will be given to us; and the government will rest on His shoulders; and His name will be called Wonderful Counselor. Mighty God, Eternal Father, Prince of Peace" (Isa. 9:6).

When the angel Gabriel appeared to Mary he said that the baby she would bear "will be great and will be called the Son of the Most High; and the Lord God will give Him the throne of His father David; and He will reign over the house of Jacob forever, and His kingdom will have no end"(Luke 1:32-33).

The genealogies presented in the gospels show Jesus' right to sit on David's throne. Matthew shows his legal right to David's throne (Matt. 1:1-17), while Luke shows his physical/blood right to the throne (Luke 3:23-37).

When the wise men came to Jerusalem and spoke to Herod their question was "where is he who has been born king of the Jews?" (Matt. 2:2).

The Jews had asked the prophet Samuel to give them a king like the other nations (1 Sam. 8:6). In doing so they were rejecting God from being king over them (1 Sam. 8:7). Now God the Son will rule over all creation.

CHRIST'S KINGDOM

His Will Be A Universal Kingdom

"Yours, O Lord, is the greatness and the power and the glory and the victory and the majesty, indeed everything that is in the heavens and the earth; Yours is the dominion, O Lord, and you exalt Yourself as head over all" (1 Chron. 29:11). The universal kingdom includes all that exists (Psalm 103:19-22).

His Is A Mediatorial Kingdom

Paul wrote Timothy, "there is one God and one mediator also between God and man, the man Christ Jesus" (1 Tim. 2:5). At the present time Jesus is our advocate with our Heavenly Father (1 John 2:1); representing us to Him. When Jesus comes to rule he will speak and act for the Godhead and represent the people before God. During that time we will see our mediator and live under His righteous rule.

His Is A Millennial Kingdom

Six times in Revelation 20 the phrase "one thousand years" is stated. The devil is bound for a thousand years (v.2); the devil is sealed in the abyss for a thousand years (v.3); the Tribulation martyrs are resurrected and reign with Christ for a thousand years (v.4); the rest of the dead are not resurrected until the thousand years are over (v.5); Christ reigns for a thousand years (v.6); Satan is released after a thousand years (v.7). For one thousand years Jesus will rule all creation!

Nature of Christ's Kingdom

1. It will be primarily spiritual; governed by, permeated by the Holy Spirit

    It will provide God's righteousness to sinners (Jer. 23:5-6); God said he would give a new heart and new spirit (Ezek. 36:26-38); will bring acknowledgement of Jehovah as the one true God (Zech. 8:20-23); will bring inward harmony with God's rule (Jer. 31:33); will bring about a direct knowledge of God (Jer. 31:34); will bring outpouring of God's Spirit on all flesh (Joel 2:28).

2. It will be ethical

   Inequalities of life will be adjusted (Isa. 40:4; Psalm 73:17); people will be held accountable for their actions (Jer. 31:28-30).

3. It will be social

   War will be eliminated (Zech. 9:10); will usher in eternal peace (Isa. 9:7).

4. It will be physical

   Healing of physical ills (Isa. 33:24; 34:5-6); restoration to long life (Isa. 65:20, 22); geological and climate changes (Zech. 14:3-4, 10; Isa. 4:5-6; 32:15-16); changes in the animal world (Hosea 2:18; Isa. 11:6-9; 65:25).

5. It will be political in its effects

   Jerusalem will be its center (Micah 4:3); there will be peace and security (Isa. 32:18); Israel restored to her land (Amos 9:14-15)

6. It will be ecclesiastical (religiously legalized and institutionalized)

   There will be a central sanctuary on earth (Ezek. 37:26-28); return of the Shekinah glory (Ezek. 43:1-7); universal worship of God (Isa. 66:23); compulsory worship of God (Zech. 14:16-19).

<u>Eternal future of the Kingdom</u>

1 Cor. 15:24-26 "Then comes the end, when He hands over the kingdom to the God and Father, when He has abolished all rule and all authority and power. For He must reign until He has put all His enemies under His feet. The last enemy that will be abolished is death." From then on, throughout all eternity, the kingdom of Christ will be included in the Universal Kingdom of God!

REVIEW AND REFLECTION QUESTIONS

Pre-existence and Incarnation of Christ

1. In what ways is Jesus' pre-existence recorded in the Old Testament?
2. In what ways is Jesus' pre-existence recorded in the New Testament?
3. What is the incarnation of Christ? What key New Testament passage presents it?
4. Give 4 reasons for the necessity of Christ's incarnation.
5. What two Old Testament passages speak about the virgin birth of Christ? Give at least 4 New Testament passages that are direct evidence for Jesus' virgin birth.

Humanity and Deity of Christ

1. How do we know Jesus was human? How does Scripture present him as human?
2. Why are Jesus' names and attributes important in describing and proving His deity?
3. Why are Jesus' works and claims he made about himself important in describing and proving His deity?

Person of Christ and Sacrificial Death of Christ

1. What is the hypostatic union in Christ, and what is the result of it?
2. What 3 primary Old Testament references predict Christ's sacrificial death?
3. Give 3 times Jesus specifically told His disciples of His coming death and resurrection.
4. Why did Jesus have to die?

5.   The terms substitutionary sacrifice, reconciliation, propitiation, and redemption are all used in reference to Jesus' sacrifice. Why are they important in your relationship to and fellowship with God?

Resurrection and Ascension of Christ

1.   What specific predictions of Jesus' resurrection are found in the Old Testament?
2.   Give at least 5 times Jesus spoke of his coming resurrection.
3.   Give 4 significant results of Christ's resurrection.
4.   Who saw Jesus after his resurrection, and why is that important to you?
5.   Give 4 reasons why Jesus' ascension was important.

Return and Reign of Christ

1.   Briefly explain the various views concerning the time of the rapture with reference to the tribulation period.
2.   What is the Judgment Seat of Christ and the Marriage Supper of the Lamb?
3.   What will happen when Jesus physically returns at the end of the tribulation period?
4.   Describe Christ's coming reign after the Tribulation ends.

THE HOLY SPIRIT

When the apostle Paul was imprisoned in Rome awaiting trial before the Roman emperor, A. D. 61-63, he wrote three letters to churches and one letter to an individual. These letters are known as the Prison Epistles. One of these letters, the letter to the church in Ephesus, places great emphasis on the work of the Holy Spirit. The letter to this church focuses upon God's purpose in establishing and completing His body, the church. The first three chapters of the letter speak about who we are in Christ, and the last three chapters about how we are to live for Christ. Foundational to these two main components is the role of the Holy Spirit.

In this letter Paul tells his readers the Holy Spirit seals us, guaranteeing our salvation (1:13), and gives believers access to God (2:18). Jews and Gentiles are built together into a dwelling for the Holy Spirit (2:22). The Holy Spirit reveals the mystery of Christ (3:5) and strengthens us (3:16). He brings unity between believers (4:3) because there is only One Holy Spirit (4:4). We are not to grieve the Holy Spirit (4:30) but to be filled with Him (5:18). Finally Paul tells his readers that part of the armor believers daily need is the "sword of the Spirit"- the Word of God (6:17), and that we are to "pray at all times with all prayer and petition in the Spirit" (6:18).

Clearly, the Holy Spirit is absolutely involved in the salvation and walk of God's children, as well as every other part of God's work from creation throughout eternity. Yet, when considering the persons and work of the individual members of the Godhead, the One least understood is the Holy Spirit. While we have extensive knowledge about God the Father and God the Son, when it comes to the Holy Spirit that knowledge is often lacking, and that which is there is at times confused or in error. That lack of knowledge and understanding, that confusion is not because God has not given extensive instruction concerning the personality, presence, power and priority of the Holy Spirit. He has given that information and instruction, and it behooves us to look and listen carefully to what the Holy Spirit teaches us about Himself as we study and meditate upon the Word of God.

One Bible commentator, Dr. Charles Ryrie, has described Him as 'the antidote for every error, the power for every weakness, the victory for every defeat, the supply for every need, and the answer for every question" (Charles Ryrie, The Holy Spirit, p.11). Careful study of God's Word will help us to correctly understand who He is, what He does, and what He seeks to do in and through our lives.

NATURE OF THE HOLY SPIRIT

HE IS A PERSON

One of the ancient attacks on the Holy Spirit denies His personality. This attack was by Paul of Samosata in the 3rd century A.D. and by Socinus, the founder of modern Unitarianism. A second attack, denying His deity, was by Arius (A.D. 300), who believed, "the Father created the Son, and the Son created the Spirit who was a person, but not God."

The Council of Nicea (A.D. 325) to correct this heresy adopted this statement about the Holy Spirit: "I believe in the Holy Spirit, the Lord and giver of life, who proceedeth from the Father and Son, who with the Father and Son together is worshipped and glorified; who spake by the prophets."

Jehovah's Witness doctrine today is Socinian with reference to the Holy Spirit and Arian with reference to Christ. While some religious groups and cults today continue to deny the personhood of the Holy Spirit, He is a person just as the Father and the Son are persons.

HE HAS ALL THE DISTINGUISHING MARKS OF PERSONALITY

1. Life

    John 7:37-39 Jesus said, "if anyone is thirsty, let him come to me and drink. He who believes in Me, as the Scripture said, 'from his innermost being will flow rivers of living water.' But this He spoke of the Spirit."

    2 Cor. 3:3 "You are a letter of Christ, cared for by us, written not with ink but with the Spirit of the living God, not on tablets of stone but on tablets of human hearts."

2. Intelligence

    1 Cor. 2:11 "For who among men knows the thought of a man except the spirit of the man which is in him? Even so the thoughts of God no one knows except the Spirit of God."

    Rom. 8:26-27 the Spirit intercedes for us with groanings that cannot be uttered. He knows what to pray for.

3. Purpose and Freedom

    1 Cor. 12:11 Speaking of distribution of Spiritual gifts, "but one and the same Spirit works all these things, distributing to each one individually just as He wills."

4. Activity; He does what a person does

    He speaks (Acts 8:29); he intercedes (Rom. 8:26); he commands (Acts 13:2); he performs miracles (Acts 8:39); he teaches (John 14:26; 1 Cor. 2:13); he testifies (John

15:26); he convinces and reproves (John 16:7-8); he restrains (Gen. 6:3); he commissions to Christian service (Acts 13:2,4).

5. Self-consciousness

1 Cor. 2:11 "the thoughts of God no one knows except the Spirit of God."

6. Emotion

Isa. 63:10 when God's people rebelled they grieved the Holy Spirit; Eph. 4:30 we are not to grieve the Holy Spirit; Rom. 15:30 the Holy Spirit loves.

Because of where the Holy Spirit is and the specific work that He does in the Church and lives of believers, He, of the three members of the Godhead, has the most personal contact with mankind. As a person He can and does the actions a Divine Person (God) does. As a person the Holy Spirit can be obeyed (Acts 10:19-21), lied to (Acts 5:3), resisted (Acts 7:51), grieved (Eph. 4:30), reverenced (Psalm 51:11), blasphemed (Matt. 12:31), outraged (Heb. 10:29).

CHRIST SPOKE OF THE HOLY SPIRIT AS A PERSON

1. Jesus called Him the Comforter

John 14:16-17 Another comforter (*paraklytos*- Grk; "one called alongside")- another like Jesus.

2. Jesus referred to Him as a person

John 16:13-14 "when He, the Spirit of Truth, is come..."

ASSOCIATED WITH FATHER AND SON TO INDICATE PERSONALITY

Matt. 28:19 "Baptizing them in the name of the Father and the Son and the Holy Spirit."

2 Cor. 13:14 "The grace of the Lord Jesus Christ, and the love of God, and the fellowship of the Holy Spirit, be with you all."

HE IS GOD

The Holy Spirit is not a product of God's creation or a force as some have stated. He is not simply a helper whom God uses to accomplish certain things. The Holy Spirit is a Person who possesses the divine nature, which makes Him to be God.

HE IS CALLED GOD

When Ananias and Sapphira were questioned, the apostle Peter said "why has Satan filled your heart to lie to the Holy Spirit... you have not lied to men but to God" (Acts 5:3-4). The apostle Paul, speaking of the work of the Holy Spirit in placing people into the body of Christ and giving them spiritual gifts said, "but now God has placed the members, each one of them, in the body, just as He desired" (1 Cor. 12:18).

HE HAS THE ATTRIBUTES OF GOD

In addition to being equal in personhood with the other members of the Godhead, the Holy Spirit has all the attributes of God. The Holy Spirit has eternality (Heb. 9:14), omnipresence (Psalm 139:7; 1 Cor. 6:19), omnipotence (Job 33:4; Psalm 104:30; Gen. 1:2), omniscience (1 Cor. 2:10-12; John 16:13), truthfulness (John 14:17; 15:26; 16:13; 1 John 2:27; 5:6), holiness (Rom. 1:4; Luke

11:13), righteousness (Rom. 8:4), grace (Heb. 10:29), love (Rom. 5:5; 15:30); and sovereignty (1 Cor. 12:11; Acts 10:19-20).

HIS RELATION TO THE OTHER MEMBERS OF THE TRINITY

God (Father, Son, Holy Sprit) have existed from all eternity. Jesus said to His apostles in the Upper Room the night of his arrest, "I will ask the Father and he will give you another helper, that he may be with you forever; that is the Spirit of truth" (John 14:16). Further he said, "the Helper, the Holy Spirit, whom the Father will send in My name, He will teach you all things, and bring to your remembrance all that I said to you" (John 14:26). Theologians speak of the Holy Spirit proceeding from the Father through the Son: God the Father sent the Holy Spirit at Jesus' request.

DESIGNATIONS OF
THE HOLY SPIRIT

There are many ways in which the Holy Spirit is designated in Scripture. There are designations describing His relationships within the Godhead, those describing His attributes, and those describing His works.

THOSE DESCRIBING HIS RELATIONS WITHIN THE GODHEAD

To the Father: He is called the Spirit of God (Matt. 3:16), Spirit of our God (1 Cor. 6:11), Spirit of the Lord (Isa. 59:19), Spirit of your Father (Matt. 10:20), Spirit of the Living God (2 Cor. 3:3), and Spirit of the Lord God (Isa. 61:1).

To the Son: He is called the Spirit of Christ (Rom. 8:9), Spirit of Jesus Christ (Phil. 1:19), Spirit of His Son (Gal. 4:6).

THOSE DESCRIBING HIS ATTRIBUTES

He is called One Spirit (Eph. 4:4), the Lord the Spirit (2 Cor. 3:18), eternal Spirit (Heb. 9:14), Spirit of glory and of God (1 Peter 4:14), Spirit of life (Rom. 8:2), Spirit of holiness (Rom. 1:4), Spirit of wisdom and revelation (Eph. 1:17), Spirit of truth (John 14:17), and Spirit of grace (Heb. 10:29).

THOSE DESCRIBING HIS WORKS

He is called the Spirit of adoption (Rom. 8:15), Spirit of faith (2 Cor. 4:13), Comforter or Helper (John 14:16), the Anointing (1 John 2:27). During Jesus' millennial rule he will be the "Spirit of wisdom and understanding, Spirit of counsel and strength, Spirit of knowledge and the fear of the Lord" (Isa.11:2).

WORK OF THE HOLY SPIRIT

When considering the work of God we have seen that all three Person of the Godhead are involved. All participate in Creation, sovereign rule, covenants, salvation, and judgment. At the same time, individual members of the Godhead have works that are distinctly theirs.

WORK IN RELATION TO THE MATERIAL UNIVERSE

CREATION

The Holy Spirit worked with the other members of the Godhead in Creation. "In the beginning God created the heavens and the earth. ..the Spirit of God was moving over the surface of the waters" (Gen 1:1-2). "By His Spirit he hath garnished the heavens" (Job 26:13, KJV). See also Psalm 33:6; Isa 40:12-14.

PROCESSES OF NATURE

Destructive Processes

He is involved in destructive processes. Isa. 40:7 "The grass withers, the flower fades, because the spirit of the Lord blows upon it " (KJV). The NASB translates this "breath of the Lord."

Renewal Process

The Holy Spirit is involved in the renewal cycle of life. Psalm 104:29-30 speaking of the vast sea life, "You hide Your face, they are dismayed; You take away their spirit, they expire and return to their dust. You send forth Your Spirit, they are created; and You renew the face of the ground."

Procreative Process

When God made Adam we are told "then the Lord God formed man of dust from the ground, and breathed into his nostrils the breath of life, and man became a living soul" (Gen. 2:7). God made the man from the dust of the ground; God gave him life. The psalmist said of God, "You formed my inward parts; You wove me in my mother's womb" (Psalm 139:13).

Job said "the Spirit of God has made me, and the breath of the Almighty gives me life" (Job 33:4). When Mary asked how she was going to give birth to a son, since she was a virgin, the angel Gabriel told her, "the Holy Spirit will come upon you, and the power of the Most High will overshadow you; and for that reason the holy Child shall be called the Son of God" (Luke 1:35).

When conception takes place two tiny cells (one sperm and one ovum) join together and a new life, a new person, comes into existence at that instant in time. From the moment of conception this new life has a soul. Where does the soul come from? It does not come from the individual cells nor from the fertilized ovum; it comes from God. God is the one who made man a living soul. The Holy Spirit, who made Jesus a living soul, is the one, who this writer believes, creates the soul in every human being.

WORK IN RELATION TO THE SCRIPTURES

HOLY SPIRIT IS THE AUTHOR OF SCRIPTURE

God could have written His Word Himself, but He chose 40 different men over 1,600 years to write and compile his special written revelation to us. One of those men was King David, who said, "the Spirit of the Lord spoke by me, and His word was on my tongue" (2 Sam. 23:2).

While men physically wrote Scripture, the Holy Spirit was One who inspired the human author. Peter, the apostle tells us, "no prophecy was ever made by an act of human will, but men moved by the Holy Spirit spoke from God" (2 Peter 1:21).

The New Testament attributes many Old Testament Scriptures to the Holy Spirit. See Matt. 22:43 with Psalm 110; Acts 1:16 with Psalm 41:5-9; Acts 4:25 with Psalm 2:1; Heb. 3:7-11 with Psalm 95:7-11; and Heb. 10:15-16 with Jer. 31:33-34.

The New Testament attributes its words to the Holy Spirit. See 1 Cor. 2:13; John 16:12-13; Rev. 2:7.

HOLY SPIRIT IS THE TEACHER AND INTERPRETER OF SCRIPTURE

Not only is the Holy Spirit the author of Scripture, but He is the One who teaches us what it says. Jesus said, "when He, the Spirit of truth, comes, He will guide you into all the truth" (John 16:13). God, the author of His Word, teaches us what He has said!

Not only does He teach us, but He helps us to understand what He has said. This is seen in these words by the apostle Paul, "we have received the Spirit who is from God, so that we may know the things freely given to us by God, which things we also speak, not in words taught by human wisdom, but in those taught by the Spirit, combining spiritual thought with spiritual words" (1 Cor. 2:12-13).

Christians are not at the mercy of any teachers. We have the objective, authoritative Scripture as our source of instruction and the Holy Spirit as our teacher. The One who wrote the Word of God is the one who helps us to understand those words. God wants us to know and love Him as much He knows and loves us, and for that to be a reality God the Holy Spirit helps us to understand all that He has written!

WORK IN PEOPLE IN OLD TESTAMENT TIMES

RESTRAINING SIN

He strove generally with man about sin, as seen in these words about Noah's time: "my Spirit shall not strive with man forever, because he also is flesh" (Gen. 6:3). While the Holy Spirit spoke to men's hearts and consciences, they did not always listen; "You bore with them for many years, and admonished them by Your Spirit through Your prophets, yet they would not give ear, therefore You gave them into the hand of the peoples of the lands" (Neh. 9:30).

SELECTIVE INDWELLING

The Holy Spirit was not given to all of God's people. It was given to accomplish God's will and purpose in and through the person to whom He had given the Holy Spirit. Pharaoh recognized it in Joseph (Gen. 41: 28; 50:20) as did the Queen mother in Babylon in Daniel (Daniel 5:11-12).

EQUIPPING FOR SPECIAL SERVICE

For Governing Nations

God had placed the Holy Spirit in Joshua, and Moses was to commission him to lead the nation of Israel as they crossed the Jordan River into the Promised Land (Num. 27:15-23).

For Military Leadership

The Spirit of the Lord came upon Othniel the son of Kenaz to judge Israel (Judges 3:9-10). The Spirit of the Lord came upon Gideon to lead the Israelites against the Midianites and Amalekites (Judges 6:34-36).

For Feats of Physical Strength

Though he failed miserably at the end, Samson is such a clear picture of this. The Spirit of the Lord came upon him, and he killed a lion with his bare hands (Judges 14:6); at another time with the jawbone of a donkey he killed 1,000 Philistine men (Judges 15:14-15).

For Artistic Work

For the skilled work needed for the Tabernacle God had filled Bezalel and Oholiab with the Holy Spirit and gave them the skills they would need (Exod. 31:4-5).

For Literary and Musical Expression

King David said that the Spirit of the Lord spoke by him, and His Word was on his tongue; the God of Israel said and spoke to him (2 Sam. 23:1-3).

<u>For Moral and Spiritual Courage</u>

The Spirit of the Lord came on Zechariah the son of Jehoiada the priest, and he spoke out against the rulers and king of Judah who had turned away from God. He was stoned to death in the courtyard of the temple (2 Chron. 24:20-22).

<u>For Prophetic Ministry and Writing of Scripture</u>

The Holy Spirit came upon Balaam when King Balak was trying to get him to curse Israel (Num. 24:2). The Holy Spirit lifted Ezekiel in a vision and carried him to the east gate of the Temple and then to the exiles in Chaldea (Ezek. 11:5, 24-25).

These special works of the Holy Spirit in the Old Testament were not for all Old Testament saints. They were not always related to moral and spiritual character, as seen in His presence in Samson, Balaam, and Saul. His presence was not always permanent; seen in David's prayer that God would not take His Holy Spirit from him (Psalm 51:11).

LIMITATIONS OF THE HOLY SPIRIT'S MINISTRY IN THESE

It was limited in extent. Not all were given the Holy Spirit, and not all received the benefits.

It was limited in duration. It could be withdrawn, as seen in Samson and Saul.

It was limited in effect. Neh. 9:20 and Isa. 63:10-11, 14 speak of a general ministry of the Holy Spirit to the nation. While the whole nation would benefit from His being given, the Holy Spirit was not given universally.

WORK IN THE LIFE OF JESUS CHRIST

CONCEPTION AND BIRTH

The angel Gabriel appeared to Mary, saying, "the Holy Spirit will come upon you, and the power of the Most High will overshadow you; and for that reason the holy Child shall be called the Son of God" (Luke 1:35). An angel told her betrothed husband, Joseph, the same thing, "Joseph, son of David, do not be afraid to take Mary as your wife; for the Child who has been conceived in her is of the Holy Spirit" (Matt. 1:20). The writer of Hebrews said that the Father prepared a body for Jesus (Heb. 10:5) and that Jesus Himself took on flesh and blood so that he could defeat Satan and set people free from his deadly hold (Heb. 2:14–15).

The agent, the One who made this conception and birth possible, was the Holy Spirit. The result of this conception was the Incarnation; God who had made mankind had now taken upon Himself a sinless human nature. The Second Person of the Triune God, not ceasing to be God, had now also become man. He was now the God–Man. Jesus in his humanity

GROWTH AND DEVELOPMENT

No indication is mentioned in Scripture concerning Jesus' relationship to the Holy Spirit as He grew up and lived in Nazareth. Luke gives two clues to Jesus' development and knowledge in the early years. The first is during his early childhood: "the Child continued to grow and become strong, increasing in wisdom; and the grace of God was upon Him" (Luke 2:40). The second was when He was twelve years old celebrating the Passover in Jerusalem with his parents. There Jesus said to Joseph and Mary who had been looking for him, "why is it that you were looking for Me? Did you now know that I had to be in My Father's house?" (Luke 2:49). These two incidents strongly imply the working of the Holy Spirit in his heart and life during these years.

Nothing else is heard about Jesus from age twelve until He is baptized by John the Baptist. At His baptism God spoke from heaven, "this is My beloved Son, in whom I am well-pleased" (Matt. 3:17). He had lived a sinless life through all those years (2 Cor. 5:21a; Heb. 4:15), and as He begins his ministry God the Father gives His affirmation of His life and now His ministry.

HIS MINISTRY

He Was Anointed with the Spirit at His Baptism

Matt. 3:16-17 "After being baptized, Jesus came up immediately from the water; and behold, the heavens were opened, and he saw the Spirit of God descending as a dove and lighting on Him, and behold, a voice out of the heavens said, 'This is My beloved Son, in whom I am well-pleased.'" See also Mark 1:9-11 and Luke 3:21-23 accounts of Jesus' baptism.

1. This was the confirmation to John the Baptist that Jesus was the Messiah and the Son of God. God had told him, "He upon whom you see the Spirit descending and remaining upon Him, this is the One who baptizes in the Holy Spirit" (John 1:33). John's response, "I myself have seen, and have testified that this is the Son of God" (John 1:34).
2. This is the fulfillment of the Messianic prophecies stating that the Servant of the Lord would be filled with the Holy Spirit.

Isa. 42:1 "Behold, My Servant, whom I uphold; My chosen one in whom My soul delights. I have put My Spirit upon Him; He will bring forth justice to the nations."

Isa. 61:1 "the Spirit of the Lord God is upon me, because the Lord has anointed me to bring good news to the afflicted; He has sent me to bind up the brokenhearted, to proclaim liberty to captives and freedom to prisoners."

3. This was the special empowerment for His public ministry of preaching, healing, casting out demons.

Acts 10:38 "You know of Jesus of Nazareth, how God anointed Him with the Holy Spirit and with power, and how He went about doing good and healing all who were oppressed by the devil, for God was with Him."

Luke 4:16-21 When Jesus came to Nazareth He entered the synagogue and read Isaiah 61:1 to those gathered to worship. Closing the scroll he said, "today this Scripture has been fulfilled in your hearing" (v.21).

His preaching was with power and authority (Luke 4:18, 22, 32, 36). He cast out demons by the Spirit of God (Matt. 12:28). He displayed great wisdom and understanding (Isa. 11:2; John 7:15). Throughout His entire ministry Jesus was empowered by the Holy Spirit. Some of His miracles were done in His own power, such as the woman with the issue of blood (Mark 5:30), healing of the paralytic (Luke 5:17-26), mass healing after choosing His disciples (Luke 6:19). Also in His own power was the effect of His words "I am" when confronted with the soldiers in the Garden of Gethsemane (John 18:6). The best statement to make is Jesus did some of his miracles in His own power and some in the power of the Holy Spirit.

He Was Filled with the Holy Spirit

Luke 4:1 "Jesus, full of the Holy Spirit, returned from the Jordan and was led around by the Spirit in the wilderness for forty days, being tempted by the devil."

John 3:34 John the Baptist, speaking about Jesus to his disciples said, "He whom God has sent speaks the words of God, for He gives the Spirit without measure."

He Was Led by the Holy Spirit

Mark 1:12 "Immediately the Spirit impelled Him to go out into the wilderness." Jesus' confrontation with the devil at the beginning of His ministry was specifically directed by the Holy Spirit. Jesus was tempted at the beginning of his ministry, throughout his ministry, and even during his sacrifice on the cross. Throughout all he never sinned. "We do not have a high priest who cannot sympathize with our weaknesses, but One who has been tempted in all things as we are, yet without sin" (Heb. 4:15).

HIS DEATH

Heb. 9:14 "How much more will the blood of Christ, who through the eternal Spirit offered Himself without blemish to God, cleanse your conscience from dead works to serve the living God?"

Throughout His life Jesus had been led, guided, filled, empowered, sustained by the Holy Spirit. When Jesus Christ left heaven to take upon himself human flesh, it was to be the sacrifice for mankind's sin. As He hung in agony on Calvary's cross, He was sustained and helped in his humanness by the Holy Spirit.

HIS RESURRECTION

Rom. 1:4 Jesus "was declared the Son of God with power by the resurrection from the dead, according to the Spirit of holiness."

Rom. 8:11 "But if the Spirit of Him who raised Jesus from the dead dwells in you, He who raised Christ Jesus from the dead will also give life to your mortal bodies through His Spirit who dwells in you."

All three Persons of the Godhead were involved in Jesus' resurrection. In addition to the Holy Spirit Jesus and the Father were part of Christ's resurrection. Jesus: "for this reason the Father loves me, because I lay down My life so that I may take it again. No one has taken it away from me, but I lay it down on My own initiative. I have authority to lay it down, and I have authority to take it up again. This commandment I received from My Father" (John 10:17-18). God the Father: "God has fulfilled this promise to our children in that he raised up Jesus, as it is also written in the second Psalm, 'You are My Son; today I have begotten You" (Acts 13:33). See also Gal. 1:1 and Eph. 1:17-20.

WORK IN RELATION TO THE CHURCH

During the year that Jesus was focusing his attention on training the twelve apostles he brought them to the area of Caesarea Philippi. There he would show them the statues to the many false gods who were worshipped there at the base of Mount Hermon, as well as the temple to Pan that had been built at that location. There, after asking them "who do you say that I am?" and Peter's answer, "Thou art the Christ, the Son of the living God" (Matt. 16:15-16). Jesus said, "upon this rock I will build My church, and the gates of Hades shall not overpower it" (Matt. 16:18).

In the Upper Room on the night of His arrest Jesus said to the twelve apostles, "I will ask the Father, and He will give you another Helper, that He may be with you forever; that is the Spirit of truth, whom the world cannot receive, because it does not see him or know Him, but you know Him because he abides with you and will be in you" (John 14:16-17). Jesus further said about this Helper, the Holy Spirit, "He will teach you all things and bring to your remembrance all that I said to you" (John 14:26). Further, "He will testify about Me" (John 15:26), and "when He comes He will convict the world concerning sin and righteousness and judgment" (John 16:8).

Forty days after His resurrection Jesus stood on the Mount of Olives with his disciples. He told them not to leave Jerusalem until they received what the Father had promised and which He had already told them about, the Holy Spirit (Acts 1:4). Jesus then said, "John baptized with water, but you will be baptized with the Holy Spirit not many days from now" (Acts 1:5). Ten days later on the Feast of Pentecost that promise would be fulfilled!

Jesus had said that he was going to build His church, and Satan would not be able to stop Him. The way and means through which He was going to do this was with the Helper that the Father was going to send: the Holy Spirit. It was His teaching, reminding, convicting work that would bring people to faith in Jesus Christ; forming the church-the body of Christ!

CHURCH CREATED BY THE HOLY SPIRIT

The Holy Spirit convicts people, drawing them to faith in Jesus Christ

Acts 2:1-4 On the Day of Pentecost, when the Twelve were together, the Holy Spirit came and filled all of them. They began to speak with other tongues as the Spirt was giving them utterance" (v.4). After preaching the message of Christ to them, Peter called them to repent, be baptized in the name of Jesus Christ for the forgiveness of their sins and receive the gift of the Holy Spirit (v.38). Three thousand people turned in faith to Jesus Christ that day, and the Church was begun.

The Holy Spirit places us into the Church, the body of Christ

1 Cor. 12:12-13 "For even as the body is one and yet has many members, and all the members of the body, though they are many, are one body, so also is Christ. For by one Spirit we were all baptized into one body, whether Jews or Greeks, whether slaves or free, and we were all made to drink of one Spirit."

CHURCH INDWELT BY THE HOLY SPIRIT

1 Cor. 3:16-17 Speaking of the Corinthian church, Paul said, "do you not know that you are a temple of God and that the Spirit of God dwells in you? If any man destroys the temple of God, God will destroy him, for the temple of God is holy, and that is what you are."

Eph. 2:19-22 The church is "built on the foundation of the apostles and prophets, Christ Jesus Himself being the cornerstone, in whom the whole building, being fitted together, is growing into a holy temple in the Lord, in whom you also are being built together into a dwelling of God in the Spirit." The indwelling Holy Spirit is the One doing the work which has Jesus Christ as its foundation.

CHURCH PRESIDED OVER BY THE HOLY SPIRIT

Holy Spirit Governs the Church

1. He appoints overseers- Acts 20:28 "Be on guard for yourselves and for all the flock, among which the Holy Spirit has made you overseers, to shepherd the church of God which He purchased with His own blood."
2. He gives gifts- (1 Cor. 12:1-11). These are given for the common good (v.7), distributed as the Holy Spirit chooses (v.11).
3. He calls the church to listen to His voice-(Rev. 2:7, 11, 17, 29; 3:6, 13, 22).

Holy Spirit Preaches the Word of God

Acts 4:8-12 "then Peter, filled with the Holy Spirit, said to them ... there is salvation in no one else; for there is salvation in no one else; for there is no other name under heaven that has been given among men, by which we must be saved."

1 Peter 1:12 "It was revealed to them that they were not serving themselves, but you, in these things which now have been announced to you through those who preached the gospel to you by the Holy Spirit sent from heaven- things into which angels long to look."

1 Cor. 2:4 Paul said, "My message and my preaching were not in persuasive words of wisdom, but in demonstration of the Spirit and of power."

1 Thess. 1:5 "For our gospel did not come to you in word only, but also in power and in the Holy Spirit and with full conviction."

Holy Spirit and Prayer in the Church

Eph. 6:18 "With all prayer and petition pray at all times in the Spirit, and with this in view, be on the alert with all perseverance and petition for all the saints."

Holy Spirit and Worship

Eph. 5:18-19 "be filled with the Spirit, speaking to one another in psalms and hymns and spiritual songs, singing and making melody with your heart to the Lord."

CHURCH UNIFIED BY THE HOLY SPIRIT

There is unity in the Church because of the forgiveness of sin and eternal life in Jesus Christ for all who compose it. At the same time there is responsibility in each local assembly of the body of Christ to guard and preserve that unity; done through the ministry of the Holy Spirit in individual hearts and lives.

Eph. 4:1-3 "I implore you to walk in a manner worthy of the calling with which you have been called, with all humility and gentleness, with patience, showing tolerance for one another in love, being diligent to preserve the unity of the Spirit in the bond of peace."

CHURCH EXTENED AND COMPLETED BY THE HOLY SPIRIT

The Holy Spirit selects special workers: Acts 13:2 "The Holy Spirit said, 'set apart for Me Barnabas and Saul for the work to which I have called them.'"

The Holy Spirit sends out the workers: Acts 13:4 "So, being sent out by the Holy Spirit, they went down to Seleucia and from there they sailed to Cyprus."

The Holy Spirit chooses fields of service: Acts 16:6-7 "They passed through the Phrygian and Galatian region, having been forbidden by the Holy Spirit to speak the word in Asia; and after they came to Mysia, they were trying to go into Bithynia, and the Spirit of Jesus did not permit them."

The Holy Spirit sustains in difficult times: Acts 13:50-52 The message of Christ rejected and Paul and Barnabas driven out of Antioch of Pisidia, "the disciples were continually filled with joy and with the Holy Spirit."

The Holy Spirit gives wisdom and guidance to solve problems arising in the Church: Acts 15:28 In dealing with the issue of circumcision and salvation, James wrote, "it seemed good to the Holy Spirit and to us to lay upon you no greater burden than these essentials."

The Church would not be here apart from the Holy Spirit. He is absolutely critical in the formation, equipping, leading, operation, and message of the Church! Anything and everything the Church does must be done through the Holy Spirit!

WORK IN THE LIFE OF THE BELIEVER

HOLY SPIRIT REGENERATES THE UNSAVED MAN

Regeneration means rebirth, new birth, to be born again. It is that act of God which imparts eternal life to those who are spiritually dead (Eph. 2:4-6). Scripture clearly teaches that regeneration is the act of God. John 1:12-13 "But as many as received Him, to them He gave the right to become children of God, even to those who believe in His name, who were born, not of blood nor of the will of the flesh nor of the will of man, but of God."

Particularly and specifically regeneration is the work of the Holy Spirit. When Nicodemus came to Jesus, Jesus said that "unless one is born again, he cannot see the kingdom of God" (John 3:3). When Nicodemus asked how this could occur, Jesus said, "unless one is born of water and the Spirit he cannot enter into the kingdom of God "(v.5).

Paul gives further instruction concerning this in his letter to Titus. "But when the kindness of God our Savior and His love for mankind appeared, He saved us, not on the basis of deeds which we have done in righteousness, but according to His mercy, by the washing of regeneration and renewing by the Holy Spirit, whom He poured out upon us richly through Jesus Christ our Savior" (Titus 3:4-6).

We are saved by grace (God's unmerited favor poured out upon us) through faith (that complete trust in the atoning work of Jesus Christ on Calvary's cross). It is not something that we have earned, but it is God's gift to us. God has provided the all-sufficient sacrifice of His Lamb for our sins, and when we responded in faith to God's offer of forgiveness and eternal life in Jesus Christ, God in his grace gave us that new birth. The One who was sacrificed to pay for our sins was Jesus Christ; the One who applied that sacrifice to us was the Holy Spirit. Because of this regenerating work of the Holy Spirit, we are a new creation; "the old things passed away; behold, new things have come" (2 Cor. 5:17).

A.W. Pink describes our regeneration by the Holy Spirit: "in regeneration one of God's elect is the subject, and the Spirit of God is the sole agent. The subject of the new birth is wholly passive; he does not act, but is acted upon. This great change is not a gradual and protracted process, but is instantaneous; in an instant of time the favored subject of it passes from death unto life. In regeneration the Spirit imparts a real, new, and immortal life; a life not such as that which was inherited from the first Adam, who was a living soul, but such as is derived from the last Adam, who is a quickening Spirit... Regeneration consists of a radical change of heart, for there is implanted a new disposition as the foundation of all holy actions; the mind being renovated, the affections elevated, and the will emancipated from the bondage of sin" (Pink, Holy Spirit, ch.10).

HOLY SPIRIT BAPTIZES THE BELIEVER

The baptism of the Holy Spirit is that work in which He brings the believer into spiritual union with Jesus and with all other believers who are in Him and who are saved during this age! It is often confusing as people attempt to understand the ministries of the Holy Spirit. The possible reasons for that confusion are multiple. For some, it is blended with or confused with water baptism, which is to be that step of obedience and identification with Christ. For some, it is identifying baptism with being filled with the Spirit.

Characteristics of the Spirit's Baptizing Work

1. Jesus is the one doing the baptizing (Luke 3:16; John 1:33), using the Holy Spirit as the agent or means of baptism.
2. There is a great difference between baptism with the Holy Spirit into Christ (Gal. 3:27; Rom. 6:3) and water baptism in the name of Christ (Acts 2:38; 10:48). The only relationship between the two is that water baptism is symbolic of what occurred when the believer is baptized into Christ.

3. This baptism is universal among all believers in this age
    and occurs once at the moment of their salvation (1 Cor.
    12:13; Gal. 3:27). All are baptized with the Spirit (1 Cor.
    12:13), and there is one Lord, one faith, one baptism (Eph.
    4:5). This is not one baptism for Jews and one for gentiles;
    it is one baptism for all. Also if this baptism could be
    repeated, that would mean that a person could cease to
    be a member of the body of Christ and would need to be
    brought back in again.

Consequences of the Spirit's Baptizing Work

1. This baptism places the believer into Jesus' death, burial,
    and resurrection. Rom. 6:3-4 "Do you not know that all
    of us who have been baptized into Christ Jesus have been
    baptized into His death? Therefore we have been buried
    with Him through baptism into death so that as Christ
    was raised from the dead through the glory of the Father,
    so we too might walk in newness of life."
2. This baptism not only places the believer into Christ (Gal.
    3:27), but it places him into the spiritual body of Christ on
    earth, the Church (1 Cor. 12:13; Eph. 1:22-23; Col. 1:18).
3. The spiritual union with Jesus resulting from this baptism
    is the basis for the blessings that are the believer's (Eph.
    1:3, 7, 11; 2:6, 10; Col. 2:10-13; 1 Cor. 1:2, 30).

HOLY SPIRIT INDWELLS BELIEVERS

The indwelling of the Holy Spirit is His residing in the believer
in Christ forever. Jesus said in John 14:16-17 "I will ask the
Father, and He will give you another Helper, that he may be with
you forever, that is the Spirit of Truth, whom the world cannot
receive, because it does not see Him or know Him, but you know
Him because he abides with you and will be in you."

1. The Holy Spirit indwells each believer individually (John 14:16-17; 1 Cor. 6:19), and through them the church collectively (1 Cor. 3:16-17; 2 Cor. 6:16). Paul said of the Ephesian church, "you are no longer strangers and aliens, but you are fellow citizens with the saints, and are of God's household, having been built on the foundation of the apostles and prophets, Christ Jesus Himself being the corner stone, in whom the whole building, being fitted together, is growing into a holy temple in the Lord, in whom you also are being built together into a dwelling God in the Spirit" (Eph. 2:19-22).

2. This indwelling occurs once for all time at the moment of salvation (Rom. 8:9; Acts 5:32; 19:2; John 14:16-17).

3. The indwelling of the Holy Spirit fulfills God's promise of His gift (John 14:16-17; Rom. 5:5; Gal. 3:2; 4:6; 1 John 3:24).

4. It is impossible to be saved and not have the Holy Spirit (Rom. 8:9).

5. The bodies of believers are the sanctuary of the Holy Spirit (1 Cor. 6:19). At the same time spiritually God the Father and the Son also indwell believers (1 John 4:12-13; Col. 1:27).

6. The Holy Spirit's presence is the pledge and promise of our future blessings in Christ (2 Cor. 5:5; Eph. 1:14).

7. The indwelling and baptism of the Holy Spirit are simultaneous events; occurring at salvation (Acts 10:44-47; 11:15-16; 19:1-6).

HOLY SPIRIT SEALS AND SECURES BELIEVERS

When an ancient document was written and was stored for safekeeping or sent to someone, it was rolled up and wax melted on its edge. A signet or stamp of some type was pressed into the soft wax. This guaranteed the authenticity of the document, its sender, and authority and power if any behind it. These verses tell the believer that he is sealed by the Holy Spirit:

> 2 Cor. 1:21-22 "Now he who establishes us with you in Christ and anointed us is God, who also sealed us and gave us the Spirit in our hearts as a pledge."

> Eph. 1:13-14 "In Him, you also, after listening to the message of truth, the gospel of your salvation-having also believed, you were sealed in Him with the Holy Spirit of promise, who is given as a pledge of inheritance, with a view to the redemption of God's own possession, to the praise of His glory."

> Eph. 4:30 "Do not grieve the Holy Spirit of God, by whom you were sealed for the day of redemption."

The one who does the sealing is God, and the seal is the Holy Spirit. Every believer is sealed at the moment he receives Christ as Savior (Eph. 1:13). It is not a sealing after being saved but sealing at the moment of salvation. Every believer, when he responds in faith in Jesus Christ is sealed by God with the Holy Spirit, and with that sealing the Holy Spirit in our hearts is God's pledge that He will keep all his promises to us.

Among all the guarantees behind a seal was the meaning of security. God's sealing a Christian is to guarantee his security. That security guaranteed he was God's possession, that his salvation was guaranteed; guaranteed God's purpose to keep us until the day of redemption. The sealing of the Holy Spirit is God's promise and guarantee of eternal security for the believer!

HOLY SPIRIT FILLS BELIEVERS

Spirit filling is not the same thing as the indwelling of the Holy Spirit. The indwelling occurs at ssalvation; the filling is to occur throughout the life of the believer. Spirit filling is not the same thing as baptizing of the Holy Spirit. Baptizing of the Holy Spirit is placing the believer into the body of Christ (1 Cor. 12:13); Spirit filling is for those who are part of the body of Christ.

The command that God's gives believers to be filled with the Holy Spirit is found in Eph. 5:18, "Do not get drunk with wine, for that is dissipation, but be filled with the Spirit." The key principle in this verse is what controls the believer; is it the flesh, the carnal nature, here represented by wine, or is the Holy Spirit controlling the believer? The filling of the Holy Spirit is His actions in taking control of the believer's life; his thoughts, speech, attitudes, conduct, and works. It is absolutely necessary for the believer to experience the full extent of the Holy Spirit's ministry in his life; necessary for spiritual growth.

The filling of the Holy Spirit is not a one-time event but a continuous action that is to occur throughout the believer's life. The Greek grammar in Eph. 5:18 points this out through the use of the present tense verb; indicating continuous action.

There is no place in Scripture where believers are told to wait for the filling of the Holy Spirit or to pray for the filling of the Holy Spirit. Yet, there are some essential steps the believer is to take so that the Holy Spirit is working in all parts of his life.

1. There needs to be dedication to God; turning from the world's standards, acts, and control; changes in the things entering the believer's mind (Rom. 12:1-2).

2. There is to be turning away from sin; not only as a whole
    but also in daily life (Rom. 6). The believer is not to be
    content to sin less, but seek to be sinless. He is to "consider
    himself to be dead to sin, but alive to God in Christ
    Jesus . .. not let sin reign in his mortal body ... not go on
    presenting the members of his body to sin as instruments
    of unrighteousness; but to present himself to God as those
    alive from the dead, and his members as instruments of
    righteousness to God" (Rom. 6:11-13). Sin is to no longer
    master him.

3. There is to be a deliberate desire and choice to live daily
    under the control of the Holy Spirit. "Walk by the Spirit,
    and you will not carry out the desire of the flesh" (Gal.
    5:16). The apostle Paul said it so clearly and concisely in
    Eph. 4:22-24 (paraphrase) "stop doing the things you used
    to do, change the way you think, and begin living the
    righteous and holy life that God wants you to live." As
    the believer seeks to let the Holy Spirit control him, the
    Holy Spirit is producing the results in the believer's life;
    making him more like the Lord Jesus Christ and his life
    more usable for Christ.

HOLY SPIRIT PRODUCES FRUIT IN THE BELIEVER

The key passage that speaks about the product of the Holy Spirit's
work in the believer's life is Gal. 5:16-25. There the apostle Paul
speaks of the conflict that takes place in the believer's heart.
"Walk by the Spirit, and you will not carry out the desire of the
flesh. For the flesh sets its desire against the Spirit, and the Spirit
against the flesh; for these are in opposition to one another, so
that you may not do the things that you please" (vv.16-17). This
is a continuing battle, and at times the flesh is victorious.

Paul states that the things the flesh produces when it is in control are "immorality, impurity, sensuality, idolatry, sorcery enmities, strife, jealousy, outbursts of anger, disputes, dissensions, factions, envying, drunkenness, carousing, and things like these, of which I forewarn you" (vv.19-21a). Paul also states there the end result of those things: "those who practice such things will not inherit the kingdom of God" (v.21b). That is the end result of those who are under the Law.

If that is all that is presented this would be a very bleak and hopeless picture, but it is not! Paul said, "but if you are led by the Spirit, you are not under the Law" (v.18). In contrast to the deeds of the flesh; that which the flesh produces in the person's life, the Spirit produces something completely different. The fruit of the Spirit (the product of the Spirit's work in the believer's heart and life) is love, joy, peace, patience, kindness, goodness, faithfulness, gentleness, self-control" (vv.22-23a).

Paul's conclusion to this conflict and opposing results is the victory that is the believer's: "now those who belong to Christ Jesus have crucified the flesh with its passions and desires" (v.24). The child of God does not have to do these deeds of the flesh; his sin was nailed to the cross of Jesus Christ, and he now has a new nature and the Holy Spirit living in him. He can walk in victory over all these sinful products of the flesh. He can have the Holy Spirit producing this fruit in his heart and life! "If (since) we live by the Spirit, let us also walk by the Spirit" (v.25). Just as the Holy Spirit has given eternal life to the one who was spiritually dead, He will produce that spiritual fruit as the believer chooses to walk daily being led, controlled, filled by Him.

HOLY SPIRIT GIVES SPIRITUAL GIFTS TO BELIEVERS

Spiritual gifts are not natural abilities which a person may possess from physical birth, nor are they skills that may be perfected through usage and training. A simple definition is that a spiritual gift is a specific ability to minister to other people; given by the Holy Spirit when the person receives Christ as Savior.

Spiritual gifts are not earned, but they are given by the grace of God through the Holy Spirit of God (1 Peter 4:10). Believers have no guarantee they will receive the specific spiritual gifts they desire, and they can't direct the Holy Spirit in which gifts they are given. Spiritual gifts are given as the Holy Spirit chooses (1 Cor. 12:11).

Gifts are given to all believers; no one is excluded (1 Peter 4:10). He never gives one particular gift to all believers, nor does He give all the gifts to one believer (1 Cor. 12:8-10). Just as "the body is not one member, but many" (1 Cor. 12:14), so spiritual gifts are given to all the different members of the body of Christ.

Spiritual gifts are not given to minister to oneself but to minister to others. They are given so that believers need one another and care for one another (1 Cor. 12:25). Paul said, "but to each one is given the manifestation of the Spirit for the common good" (1 Cor. 12:7). Peter said that we are to use them in "serving others, as good stewards of the manifold grace of God" (1 Peter 4:10). God has given the spiritual gifts to be a unifying source in the church!

Spiritual gifts are listed in three different places in the New Testament; with some overlap. Eighteen gifts are stated in Rom. 12:3-8; 1 Cor. 12:8-10, 28-30; Eph. 4:11. The gifts may be classified as follows:

Speaking gifts: apostleship, prophecy, evangelism, pastoring, teaching, exhorting, word of wisdom, word of knowledge, tongues, interpretation of tongues.

Serving gifts: ministration (helps), government (ruling), giving, mercy, faith, discernment of spirits, miracles, healing.

Sign gifts: miracles, healing, tongues, interpretation of tongues.

The gifts given are permanent in the individual believer until the Lord takes them to heaven. They are here for the Church age. Some will have different lengths of duration and usefulness in the Church (1 Cor. 13:8b-10).

OTHER MINISTRIES OF THE HOLY SPIRIT TO THE BELIEVER

He Teaches The Believer

In the Upper Room, after saying that the Holy Spirit was going to come, Jesus said, "when He, the Spirit of truth, comes, he will guide you into all the truth; for He will not speak on His own initiative, but whatever he hears, he will speak, and He will disclose to you what is to come. He will glorify Me, for he will take of Mine and will disclose it to you (John 16:12-14).

The Holy Spirit teaches through what He has written (Scripture), gives the interpretation, understanding, and assists in the application of those truths. As He teaches Jesus is glorified, and the believer is edified.

He Guides the Believer

The guiding work of the Holy Spirit is a great hope and encouragement to the child of God. "For all who are being led by the Spirit of God, these are sons of God" (Rom 8:14). Not only is God's Word "a lamp to our feet and light to our path" (Psalm 119:105), but the Holy Spirit leads God's children as they listen to His directions (Acts 8:29; 10:19-20; 13:2, 4; 16:6-7; 20:22-23).

He Assures the Believer

The Holy Spirit has written that we have been sealed with the Spirit as a guarantee of our coming redemption (Eph. 1:13-14). He wrote of assurance of salvation in 1 John 5:1-13. In Rom. 8:16-17a He said "the Spirit Himself testifies with our spirit that we are children of God, and if children, heirs also, heirs of God and fellow heirs with Christ." The assurance of salvation comes from the Holy Spirit speaking to our hearts!

He Prays for the Believer

There are times when the believer is so overwhelmed with circumstances that he is not able to pray; times when he does not know what to pray; times that he does not know God's will in his prayer. At these times "the Spirit also helps our weaknesses; for we do not know how to pray as we should, but the Spirit Himself intercedes for us with groanings too deep for words; and he who searches the hearts knows what the mind of the Spirit is, because he intercedes for the saints according to the will of God" (Rom. 8:26-27). Eph. 6:18 states that the Holy Spirit guides and directs prayers.

BELIEVER'S RESPONSIBILITY TO THE HOLY SPIRIT

1. The believer is to walk according to the Spirit (Rom. 8:1, 4-5; Gal. 5:16, 25).

   Rom. 8:1, 4-5 "There is therefore now no condemnation for those who are in Christ Jesus...so that the requirement of the Law might be fulfilled in us, who do not walk according to the flesh but according to the Spirit. For those who are according to the flesh set their minds on the things of the flesh, but those who are according to the Spirit, the things of the Spirit."

   Gal. 5:16, 25 "Walk by the Spirit, and you will not carry out the desire of the flesh...If we live by the Spirit, let us also walk by the Spirit."

2. The believer is to live in the power of the Spirit (Rom. 15:13; Gal. 5:25).

   Rom. 15:13 "Now may the God of hope fill you with all joy and peace in believing, so that you will abound in hope by the power of the Holy Spirit."

3. The believer is to have the mind of the Spirit (Rom. 8:6).

    "For the mind set on the flesh is death, but the mind set on the Spirit is life and peace."

4. The believer is to pray in the Spirit (Eph. 6:18; Jude 20).

    Eph. 6:18 "With all prayer and petition pray at all times in the Spirit, and with this in view, be on the alert with all perseverance and petition for all the saints."

    Jude 20 "But you, beloved, building yourselves up on your most holy faith, praying in the Holy Spirit."

5. The believer is to keep the unity of the Spirit (Eph. 4:2-3).

    "With all humility and gentleness, with patience, showing tolerance for one another in love, being diligent to preserve the unity of the Spirit in the bond of peace."

6. The believer is to use the sword of the Spirit (Eph. 6:17b, 19).

    Eph. 6:17b The sword of the Spirit is the Word of God.

    Eph. 6:19 "Pray on my behalf, that utterance may be given to me in the opening of my mouth, to make known with boldness the mystery of the gospel."

7. The believer is to put to death the deeds of the body by the Spirit (Rom. 8:13).

    "If you are living according to the flesh, you must die; but if by the Spirit you are putting to death the deeds of the body, you will live."

8. The believer is to wait for the hope of righteousness through the Spirit (Gal. 5:5).

   "For we through the Spirit, by faith, are waiting for the hope of righteousness."

9. The believer is to work for the Spirit and not the flesh (Gal. 6:7-8).

   "Do not be deceived, God is not mocked; for whatever a man sows, this he will also reap. For the one who sows to his own flesh will from the flesh reap corruption, but the one who sows to the Spirit will from the Sprit reap eternal life."

SINS AGAINST THE HOLY SPIRIT

COMMITTED BY UNBELIEVERS

Resisting the Spirit; resisting his message, resisting his work is one sin the unbeliever commits. Stephen spoke of this when he was defending his life before the Council in the Sanhedrin (Acts 6-7). Speaking of their rejection of God's truth, he said, "you men who are stiff-necked and uncircumcised in heart and ears are always resisting the Holy Spirit; you are doing just as your fathers did" (Acts 7:51).

Insulting, treating with contempt is another sin the unbeliever commits. The writer of Hebrews stated, "anyone who has set aside the Law of Moses dies without mercy on the testimony of two or three witnesses. How much severer punishment do you think he will deserve who has trampled under foot the Son of God, and has regarded as unclean the blood of the covenant by which he was sanctified, and has insulted the Spirit of grace?" (Heb. 10:28-29). According to this, rejecting Jesus Christ is also insulting and treating with contempt the Holy Spirit. It is the Holy Spirit who is doing the convicting and pointing people to Jesus Christ.

A third sin against the Holy Spirit is blasphemy. Matt. 12:31 Jesus said, "therefore, I say to you, any sin and blasphemy shall be forgiven people, but blasphemy against the Spirit shall not be forgiven." The Jews in Matthew 12 were attributing the miraculous works that Jesus was doing to Satan and not to God; not to Jesus himself as God, nor to the Holy Spirit through whom Jesus did most of his miracles. The Holy Spirit was working and speaking in Christ, and they were saying that it was Satan who was doing these things. It was this blasphemy that caused Jesus from that point onward to speak to the Jewish religious leaders primarily in parables.

COMMITTED BY BELIEVERS

Quenching the Spirit is a sin that believers commit at times. Quenching means to stifle, suppress, even put out (as in a fire). There are often times the Holy Spirit is seeking to work in a person's life, and they are not willing to listen. The Holy Spirit is leading, and the person is not willing to follow. The apostle Paul said, "do not quench the Spirit" (1 Thess. 5:19).

Grieving the Spirit is another sin that believers commit. God's desire for the believer is to be holy, because He is holy. Part of the work the Holy Spirit does in the Christian's life is to daily make him more holy, to daily make him more like Jesus Christ. When sin, unintentional or intentional, is present in the believer's life, the Holy Spirit is grieved. Paul said, "do not grieve the Holy Spirit of God, by whom you were sealed for the day of redemption" (Eph. 4:30).

A third sin committed by believers against the Holy Spirit is lying. That is what Ananias and Sapphira had done and were judged for doing so (Acts 5:3). God knows everything (Psalm 139:1-6); why would a believer lie to God, but that often happens.

Conclusion

In the beginning God created everything; at the cross God paid the sacrifice for man's sin, and to all God said, "come unto Me, you who are weary and heavy laden, I will give you rest." "The Spirit and the Bride say 'come;' let the one who hears say, 'come,' and let the one who is thirsty come; let the one who wishes take the water of life without cost!" <u>God is</u>, and therefore we have hope!

"Now to Him who is able to keep you from stumbling, and to make you stand in the presence of His glory blameless with great joy, to the only God our Savior, through Jesus Christ our Lord, be glory, majesty, dominion and authority, before all time and now and forever" (Jude 24-25).

AMEN! AMEN! AMEN!
EVEN SO QUICKLY COME, LORD JESUS!

REVIEW AND REFLECTION QUESTIONS

Nature and Designations of the Holy Spirit

1. How do we know the Holy Spirit is a person? List 4 of his marked indicators of personality.
2. How did Christ refer to the Holy Spirit in John 14 and John 16?
3. Describe the circumstances where the Holy Spirit is called God.

Work of the Holy Spirit

1. Was the Holy Spirit involved in Creation?
2. What 2 roles does the Holy Spirit have in relationship to the Word of God.
3. Describe the work of the Holy Spirit in Old Testament times.
4. What role did the Holy Spirit have in the birth of Jesus?
5. What 3 major ways was the Holy Spirit involved in and integral to the ministry of Christ?
6. What was the Holy Spirit's role in Jesus' resurrection?
7. In what ways is the Holy Spirit working in the church?
8. What is the regenerating work of the Holy Spirit?
9. What is the baptism of the Holy Spirit?
10. When do the indwelling and sealing of the Holy Spirit occur?
11. What is the filling of the Holy Spirit? Is it a one-time event, or is it continuous in our lives? To what extent can we live Spirit-filled lives today?
12. What are spiritual gifts, and how do we get them?

Responsibility to and Sin against the Holy Spirit

1. What are the believer's responsibilities to the Holy Spirit?
2. What are sins the believer can commit against the Holy Spirit?

Bibliography

Bauer, Walter; Arndt, William F., Gingrich, F. Wilbur, Danker, Frederick. *A Greek-English Lexicon of the New Testament and Other Early Christian Literature.* Chicago: University of Chicago Press, 1979.

Brown, Francis; Driver, S. R.; Briggs, Charles A. *A Hebrew and English Lexicon of the Old Testament.* Oxford: Clarendon Press, 1980.

Chafer, Lewis Sperry. *Chafer Systematic Theology.* Dallas: Dallas Seminary Press, 1980.

Flint, Annie Johnson. "He Giveth More Grace," In *Sing Joyfully Hymnal.* Carol Stream: Tabernacle Publishing, 1989, #351.

Harris, R. Laird; Archer Jr., Gleason L.; Waltke, Bruce K. *Theological Word Book of the Old Testament.* Chicago: Moody Press, 1980.

Merriam Webster's Collegiate Dictionary, 10th ed. Springfield, Mass.: Merriam-Webster, Inc., 1993.

Packer, J. I. "God Speaks to Man." In *Christian Foundations.* Philadelphia: Westminster Press, 1965, II:29.

Pink, A. W. *The Holy Spirit, Kindle Edition.* E4 Group, 2014.

Ryrie, Charles C. *The Holy Spirit*. Chicago: Moody Press, 1997.

Thomas, W. H. Griffith. *Christianity is Christ*. London: Longmans Green and Co., 1909.

Unger, Merrill F. *New Unger's Bible Dictionary*. Chicago: Moody Press, 1988.

Walvoord, John F., Zuck, Roy B. *The Bible Knowledge Commentary*. Victor Books, 1985.

Whitcomb, John (revision) of McClain, Alva. *God and Revelation: Theology Syllabus*. Winona Lake: Grace Theological Seminary, 1982.

Printed in the United States
by Baker & Taylor Publisher Services